CONTENTS

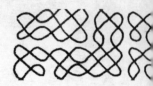

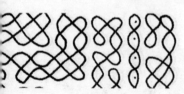

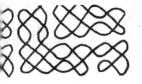

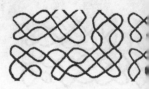

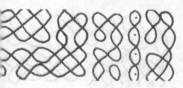

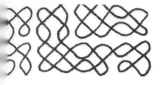

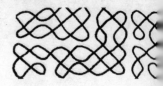

Vegetarian Curries & Fries

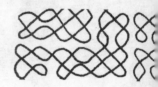

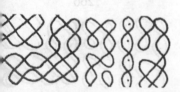

INTRODUCTION

*W*hen some acquaintances learnt that I was writing a cook book, their amazement knew no bounds! My having held parallel careers in textile designing, writing and broadcasting, they could not for the life of them, associate me with cooking. My only answer is that creativity has been the thread of commonality which has been woven into all my spheres of activity, and I do believe that one can be creative, even in cooking.

The purpose of this book is a projection of tradition rather than innovation. Having been, most of my adult life, very influenced by tradition, I have been collecting over the years, languishing and languished recipes of families who kept them as closely guarded secrets. Some of these recipes were consigned to the back drawer, some were in a state of disintegration, and the paper on which they were handwritten, yellow with age.

This was when I decided that something should be done to revive some of these precious recipes, adapting them to modern day requirements, for in most homes the fire wood stoves, the grinding stone and the giant stone mortar and pestle are obsolete. I was also motivated when the girls in my family constantly badgered me to send them recipes of some of the dishes that are part of my repertoire. I thought that nothing would be better than a handbook of traditional recipes from each state, which would be invaluable to those women who enjoy cooking traditional food, and who have no way

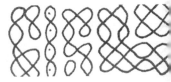

of acquiring these near extinct recipes. I confess, however, that I have tried to adapt the recipes to suit modern lifestyles, in using existing gadgets which make cooking simpler.

A beginning was made with my collection of recipes from my own family, from my mother, Leela Chander, who is a cook *par excellence,* and who believes that every detail should be just so, and will not compromise on procedures. The results certainly show, and I have worked very closely with her, getting her to check and re-check my techniques, to proof read my recipes and point out errors. Almost all of my mother's time tested recipes have been listed in this book.

I am grateful to my husband Kittu, who suffered silently my hours of insular preoccupation with this book, and who was always on hand if I needed help, and to all those who have eaten at our table and encouraged my culinary experiments!

Since recipes for Brahmin cookery are easily available, I have concentrated on the Tamilian non-Brahmin cookery, which is exotic and miles apart from the ubiquitious *sambhars, rasam, idlis* and *dosais,* though the basic dishes have also been included , being common to the Brahmin and non-Brahmin communities. Featured in this book are Mudaliar, Chettinad, Vellala Christian and other recipes common to various Tamilian communities.

The communities.....

A two hour drive from Chennai down dusty roads leads one to Vellore where the Mudaliar presence is felt. South and North Arcot districts are the strongholds of the Mudaliar community which is also scattered in Kancheepuram, Chennai and Bangalore. The Mudaliars were primarily agriculturalists and weavers, but like the Chettiars there are respected scholars and talented dramatists in the community. Sociable by nature, the Mudaliar hospitality has to be experienced to be believed. The guest is honoured and welcomed most warmly into the home. Food is of prime importance, and many of the Mudaliar men were known to discuss the day's menu with their wives, often shopping for the meat and vegetables themselves.

The *vengalam paanai* or metal vessel, was commonly used for serving food in the olden days, and copper and *kal chatti* (stone) utensils were believed to have medicinal properties. Fish curry was always made in an earthern-ware dish. It is believed that the taste improved multifold when left in it for a day or two, and tamarind being a preservative, keeps the curry from going bad. An *eeyam* vessel was a tin vessel which could not be placed directly over the fire without liquid in it! Rasam was made in a kadai and then transferred to the *eeyam* vessel for boiling. An *eeyam* vessel was used extensively for making rasam, and *kal chatti* for mashing dal or *Keerai* (Spinach). With dedicated servants in the old days, maintenance of these vessels was hardly a problem!

The South Indian diet is considered wholesome and nutritious, with the accent on the nutritive value, and the way it is cooked. The meal is very balanced when two or three of the dishes are imaginatively combined. The sambhar or vegetable kurma is ever present on vegetarian days, strictly observed by the non- vegetarian. The side dishes range from the simple *pachidi* and *poriyals* to meat and fish fries.

Tiffin dishes are internationally popular, as they are preferred to heavy meals by busy executives or the housewife who wants only a light meal at night. Most South Indians love the *papadams* and the *vathals* which are deep fried. The Tamilian loves his rice. A complete meal consists of rice as the main dish, the curry, a side dish, salad or *poriyal, rasam* and curd.

Ground *masalas* are required for most of the dishes. The *masalas* were originally hand ground on the stone, and the paste so fine that it was said to resemble satin. The old timers who have seen this kind of preparation reiterate that the dishes prepared from mixie ground *masalas* and pressure cooked, do not taste the same as those done with stone ground *masalas* and cooked over slow heat.

Originally food was served in the kitchen by the lady of the house, and family members were expected to sit on the ground on a hard plank of wood and eat off banana leaves. This imparts a special flavour to the food, and it was believed that eating, seated on the ground improved one's physical condition. The hot food placed on the banana leaf distinctly releases a pleasant flavour.

Goat meat is favoured in this community, and coconut used in many of their dishes. Mudaliar cookery is economical, very tasty, not too spicy and does not need much oil or ghee for seasoning. Mudaliars shy away from pork or beef, but eat every part of the goat. Most popular on special occasions is the *ãppam* and *ãttu kaal kozhambu* combination, ...soft, white, fluffy pancakes, eaten with thick, rich soup made from sheep's trotters. A closely guarded secret from some of the prominent Mudaliar families is *Chuppal Kari*, where meat and garnishes are strung on skewers, and gently cooked with aromatic spices. Another speciality is the *kari peratel*, a thin delicious soup like meat curry laced with dill and fenugreek leaves. *Mochakka*(a kind of shelled bean available in the South during winter) is an all time Mudaliar favourite.

Christian Vellala food is similar to that of the Mudaliars though more recently Western influences have crept in.

The Nattukottai Chettiars, another non Brahmin Tamil community, hail from Chettinad in south east Tamil Nadu. Essentially a non-vegetarian community, their non-vegetarian dishes are more popular than the vegetarian ones. Geographical conditions in Chettinad, made vegetables scarce. Local vegetables like brinjal, raw banana, spinach and root vegetables dominate the traditional vegetarian preparations. Most travelled among the trader communities, the Chettiar men were frequently out, leaving the women to manage the home and children. With time on their hands the Chettiar women established the food traditions of their community and the Chettiars are known for their generosity and indulgence to their guests, and their sumptuous repasts are mouth watering.

Spicier than Mudaliar food, the distinctive cuisine of Chettinad food has gained immense popularity of late. No recipe is complete without curry leaves, and garlic is used liberally as also *sombu* (aniseed).

There has been fun and excitement in putting this book together. It meant long hours in the kitchen, visiting veteran aunts who refused to divulge some very interesting traditional recipes, coaxing them to do so in the name of posterity, and even kidnapping a couple of old ladies for a day, in the hope that in a weak moment, culinary secrets would be out!

I have enjoyed writing this book, and I hope that the readers will enjoy trying out the recipes too!

Sabita Radhakrishna

WEIGHTS & MEASURES

𝒞ooking may be considered scientific, but I would describe it more as artistry, with individual touches making one's dishes unique. The palate fortunately makes allowances for this kind of minimal deviation ! I have given accurate measures according to traditional recipes, but variation is advised according to one's taste. Salt is such a debatable ingredient, that it is left to the reader to determine the quantity. The same goes for sugar and the degree of hotness dictated by chillies and pepper.

Most of my recipes bear cup or spoon measures, as I personally find them easier to follow rather than squint at an inaccurate weighing scale when one is in a hurry. However, I have also included equivalent weights so that you can clarify your doubts. Recipes have been standardised using metric measures. It is impossible to' measure' tamarind in its original form, or give a weight indication when the quantity is very small. The most convenient is a lime sized ball of tamarind or a marble sized one. Please note that the ball of tamarind has to be compressed to the required size to get the right amount. The quantity of tamarind may be reduced according to individual taste, as there are some people who do not like food to be too sour. These days purified concentrated pulp is sold in bottles.

When measuring by volume in spoons and cups, you should scoop up the required ingredient, and level it with a knife. Never pack the ingredient tightly into the cup, nor use a heaped measure unless mentioned. When you measure flour, gently tap the cup on a hard surface so that the flour levels, but again, do not pack it in. Use the same cup or spoon to measure the ingredients in

any one recipe. Seasoned cooks use a 'pinch' (1/8 teaspoon) or a 'handful' of say curry leaves! In this instance I have specified the number of curry leaves, which of course can be varied.

If you follow the recipe exactly as it is given, you will consistently turn out the dish as it was done traditionally. Ironically, if you wish to cook twice the amount, you should not double the quantity of the ingredients, but it should be only one and a half to one and three quarters of the quantity of each ingredient specified.

Given below are some working approximations for conversions.

Metric Imperial

1	cup	250	ml	8	fl oz		
½	cup	125	ml	4	fl oz		
¼	cup	60	ml	2	fl oz		
1	pint	600	ml				
½	tsp	3	gm				
1	tsp	5	gm				
2	tsp	10	gm	1	dsp		
3	tsp	15	gm	1	tbsp		
125	gm ($\frac{1}{8}$ kg)	4	oz (¼ lb)				
250	gm (¼ kg)	8	oz (½ lb)				
500	gm (½ kg)	16	oz (1 lb)				
1000	gm (1 kg)	32	oz (2 lbs)				
1500	gm (1½ kg)	48	oz (3 lbs)				

1 bunch of greens	4-5 cups of chopped leaves, heaped, loosely placed
1 bunch of coriander	½ cup of chopped leaves
1 medium sized coconut	2 ½ cups grated coconut
1 large onion	70 gm
1 medium sized onion	40 gm
1 small onion	15-20 gm
1 large potato	75 gm
1 medium sized potato	50 gm
1 large tomato	100 gm
1 medium size tomato	70 gm
1 small tomato	50 gm
1 pod garlic	30 flakes

ABBREVIATIONS

18

tsp	teaspoon
dsp	dessertspoon
tbsp	tablespoon
gm	gram
kg	kilogram
lt	litre
"	inch

TIFFIN VARIETIES

Tiffin or breakfast, is an important meal in a Tamil Nadu home. While the more Westernised of families have resorted to a bread and egg or a cereal breakfast, most families even today, turn out the well loved breakfast snacks, which serve as alternatives to a full fledged dinner in the deep South. Most hotels, in places like Salem, Madurai, Tirunelvelli and Coimbatore, prefer to serve *tiffin* at night, as it is light and easy to digest. Fermented rice is one of the main ingredients for the more popular breakfast dishes, and is an excellent starter for the day. *Tiffin* is partaken, generally, by traditional families, only after a bath, and only after offering morning worship or *puja*.

With a mind boggling range of kitchen devices in the market today, where the mixie and the wet grinder top the list in versatility, preparing *tiffin* is no longer drudgery. The *tawas* or griddles for making *dosais* are kept exclusively for this purpose, and the heavier, the better. They should be washed after use with hot water and soap using a sponge, and not scrubbed vigorously with an abrasive. The *dosai tawa* gets seasoned with continuous use, and becomes a precious acquisition.

Preparations for the rice based *tiffin* snacks get underway the previous day, and the dishes are made in the morning after the mixture ferments. Preparation timetables are given with respect to the tropical climate. In colder places, the prepared batter is kept longer for successful fermentation, maybe even a whole day. Assessment is done purely by practice and experience. *Idlis, dosais, aapams, iddiappams,* and *puris* are common to all the southern states of India.

Dosai making is a special art, and even some of the so called seasoned cooks are unable to turn out golden brown paper thin *dosais*. The secret lies in heat control, and not allowing the *tawa* to get too hot. Refrain from adding too much oil as it gets difficult to pour out the next *dosai* if the oil is not absorbed. When the *dosai* is done it begins to lift off by itself starting from the sides. You can allow it to brown a little longer before lowering the heat, and coaxing the dosai gently out of the *tawa* without breaking it.

Leftover batter either from *idlis* or *dosais*, can be used in a variety of ways with filling, using leftover food.

The internationally popular tiffin dishes are often preferred to heavy meals.

1. Idlis (Steamed Rice Cakes)
2. Pongal (Sweet Rice)
3. Getti Thuvaiyal (Thick Lentil Chutney)
4. Vadai (Patties)
5. (Coconut Chutney)
6. Sambhar (Lentil Curry)

Distinctive South Indian filter coffee served with traditional snacks.

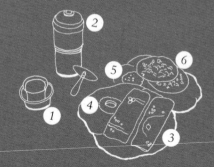

1. Coffee in Tumbler
2. Coffee Filter
3. Masala Dosai (Rice Pancakes with Savoury Filling)
4. Molagapodi (Chilli Flavoured Powder)
5. Chutney
6. Oothappam (Onion Pancakes)

FILTER KAAPI

South Indian Filter Coffee

*W*ho can resist the aroma of freshly brewed coffee early in the morning? For most South Indians the cup that cheers, means 'bed coffee' before they get on to anything else. Nothing tastes so good just then as much as filter coffee does!

Stainless steel coffee filters are the best, by way of simple equipment. There are two compartments, the upper one has holes in the base, where you need to place the coffee powder. The lower compartment receives the coffee decoction as it filters through. Then you have a plunger which consists of a steel plate with holes, connected to a thin rod in the centre which keeps the coffee powder in place, and of course you have the lid to seal in the goodness of pure coffee.

You can buy your favourite brand of coffee powder, or roast the coffee beans at home, and grind them so that it is fresh.

Our favourite combination has been : 200 gm plantation coffee+ 200 gm peaberry+ 40 gm chicory powder.

Allow two teaspoons of coffee powder per large cup, and three quarters of a cup of water per person.

Place the required amount of coffee powder in the upper compartment of the filter. Push the plunger down, to cover the coffee powder. Boil the measured quantity of water, and pour over the steel plate, in the upper compartment. Cover with the lid.

The coffee will take about 15-20 minutes to percolate completely. Heat milk and add to the coffee decoction. Add sugar to taste. A moderate amount of sugar will bring out the essence of coffee, while over addition, kills it entirely!

The 'second' decoction is prepared for those who cannot stomach strong coffee. The first decoction is removed from the lower compartment and a cup of boiling water poured into the first compartment with the plunger intact. Milk and sugar may be added the same way.

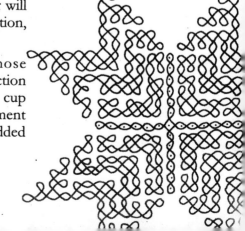

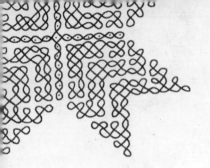

MASALA DOSAI

Rice Pancakes with Savoury Filling

3 cups	parboiled rice
1 cup	raw rice
1 cup	black gram dal
1 tsp	fenugreek seeds
	Salt to taste
	Oil for making dosais

1. Soak the two kinds of rice together in water, and the black gram dal and the fenugreek seeds together in a separate vessel, for a minimum of 5-6 hours.

2. Grind the washed black gram dal and fenugreek seeds in a wet grinder or mixie, till the mixture is smooth, light and frothy, without adding too much water.

3. Grind the two kinds of cleaned rice together into a smooth paste, and mix with the ground dal and fenugreek seeds. Add salt and mix thoroughly. Pour into a large vessel and allow to ferment overnight.

4. Mix the dosai batter thoroughly next morning and add a little water if necessary. The batter should not be runny, but on the thicker side.

5. Prepare urulakazhangu puttu (recipe page 237) and the coconut chutney as on page 56.

6. Heat an iron griddle and smear oil on it with a small piece of rolled cloth. This is not necessary if you use a non stick pan. Pour a ladle of batter in the centre of the tawa. Spread the batter with the spoon in circular movements till it forms a large thin round. Pour two teaspoons of oil around the edges. Maintain moderate heat till the dosai browns evenly. If the dosai is thin enough it is not necessary to turn it over.

7. Spread coconut (thengai) chutney right down the centre of the dosai after the dosai is cooked. Place (urulakazhangu) potato puttu along the chutney, and fold the edges so that one overlaps the other as in an omelette. Serve hot.

Serves 8

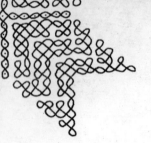

RAVA DOSAI

Semolina Pancakes

3 cups	semolina
1/3 cup	rice flour
1/4 cup	sour buttermilk
	Salt to taste
2	medium sized onions (finely chopped)
4	green chillies (finely chopped)
1/2 cup	finely chopped coriander leaves
1" piece	ginger (grated)

Seasoning

1 tsp	Oil
1 tsp	mustard seeds
1 tsp	split black gram dal
	Oil for frying

1. Mix the first 3 ingredients and allow to ferment for 6-8 hours.

2. Heat oil in a small frying pan and season with mustard seeds and split black gram dal. Add to batter. Add onions, green chillies, coriander leaves and ginger.

3. Make sure that the batter is thinner than that for masala dosais, and pour out thin dosais, as described in recipe for masala dosais, making each dosai crisp and brown.

Serve hot with coconut chutney (recipe page 56).

Serves 6

GODUMAI DOSAI

Wheat Pancakes

3 cups	wheat flour
1 ½ cups	rice flour
2 tsp	salt
¼ cup	sour buttermilk
1 large	onion
3	green chillies
½ cup	chopped coriander leaves
4	curry leaves (cut into pieces)
	Oil for frying

1. Mix the 2 types of flour with the salt and buttermilk, adding enough water to make a thin batter. Let it rest for 2 hours.

2. Chop the onion and green chillies fine, and add to batter along with coriander leaves and curry leaves.

3. Pour out dosais as usual, and serve with onion chutney (recipe page 59).

Serves 6

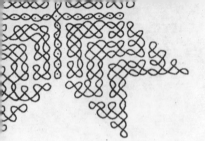

APPAM

Steamed Rice Pancakes

4 cups	raw rice
2 tbsp	parboiled rice
1 tbsp	black gram dal
1 cup	cooked rice
½ cup	fresh (grated) coconut
	Salt to taste
1 tsp	dry yeast
1 tsp	sugar
¼ cup	warm water
1	coconut
2 tsp	sugar
½ tsp	soda bicarbonate
2 tbsp	oil

1. Clean, wash and soak the first three ingredients for 4-5 hours. Drain water and grind soaked ingredients into a smooth paste, along with the cooked rice and coconut. Add salt and mix well.

2. Add warm water to the yeast and sugar and set aside for an hour or till the mixture becomes frothy. Add to the batter and mix well. Allow the mixture to ferment overnight, or for 5-6 hours.

3. Grate the whole coconut. Extract 2 cups of thick milk and ¾ cup second milk. Add the second milk to the dough along with ½ cup of thick milk with sugar. Mix the soda bicarbonate in a tablespoon of water and mix well into the dough. It should be of pouring consistency, and not as thick as dosai or idli batter.

4. Place a small iron kadai on the stove, and using a small piece of cloth, smeared with oil, grease the kadai evenly. Pour a ladle of dough into the kadai, and using both the handles, take the kadai off stove and swirl it around using a circular motion so that the batter coats the sides of the kadai. The remaining batter will settle at the bottom while the sides and ends will be lacy. Reduce the heat and cover the kadai, opening it only after the ãppam has cooked. Remove gently with a flat spoon, and repeat the process.

EGG ÃPPAM: Break an egg on to the centre of the ãppam after it is poured out and place the kadai on the stove till the ãppam is cooked. As an alternative, beat two eggs with 5 ladles of appam batter, and pour out in the usual way. The taste is enhanced and the appam takes on an attractive lemony shade.

Serve with thick coconut milk mixed with as much sugar as you prefer. Ãppams can also be served with kurmas or chutneys.

Serves 8

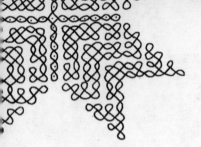

OOTHAPPAM

Onion Pancakes

4 cups	leftover dosai or idli batter
1 large	onion (finely chopped)
6	green chillies (finely chopped)
½ cup	chopped coriander leaves
1 tbsp	oil
½ tsp	mustard seeds
½ tsp	split black gram dal
	Oil for frying

1. Heat oil in a pan and season with mustard seeds and split black gram dal, and add to the batter. Mix well.

2. Pour out dosais on tawa about ¼" to $^3/_8$" thick. Sprinkle the chopped ingredients evenly. Pour a teaspoon of oil round the dosai and cover with a lid. Turn over to the other side and allow to brown.

Serve hot with any chutney.

Serves   6

ADAI

Lentil Pancakes

1 cup	raw rice
½ cup	red gram dal
½ cup	black gram dal
½ cup	Bengal gram dal
5	red chillies
1 large	onion
1 small bunch	coriander leaves
¹/₈ tsp	asafoetida powder
	Salt to taste
	Oil for frying

1. Wash the three dals and rice thoroughly, and soak for 2-3 hours, along with the red chillies.

2. Grind coarsely in a mixie.

3. Finely chop onions and coriander leaves, and add to the batter. Add asoefatida and salt and mix the batter well.

4. Pour out a thin dosai on a tawa, pour a teaspoon of oil round the sides, and cover with a lid. Turn the adai over and brown the other side.

Serve hot with coconut chutney (recipe page 56).

Serves 5

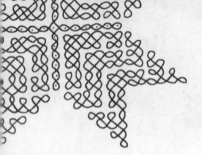

IDLI

Steamed Rice Cakes

2 cups	parboiled rice
2 cups	raw rice
1 cup	black gram dal
½ cup	cooked rice
	Salt to taste
	A pinch baking soda
	Oil for smearing moulds

1. Soak the two kinds of rice together in a vessel with water. Soak the black gram dal in water in a separate vessel, and let both soak for a minimum of 5-6 hours.

2. Thoroughly wash the black gram dal and grind adding water, till the mixture is smooth, light and frothy. Wash and grind the two varieties of rice and the cooked rice into paste without making it absolutely smooth as one does for dosais. Add salt to taste and mix thoroughly. Pour into a large vessel and allow to ferment overnight.

3. Mix the batter again in the morning, and add baking soda, first mixing it in a spoon of batter. Mix well. The batter should be thick like cake batter. Water may be added if it is too thick.

4. Smear the idli moulds with oil, and pour the batter into each of them. Steam the idlis in a pressure cooker or a steamer for about 10 minutes.

Serve hot with chutney, molagapudi or sambhar (see page numbers 56, 62, 64, 228).

Serves 6-8

KHARA IDLI

Flavoured Rice Cakes

*I*f you don't wish to eat the same kind of idlis on two consecutive days, the leftover batter can be differently flavoured, and can be had for lunch or dinner.

Add chopped onions, green chillies and coriander leaves, and season the batter with mustard seeds and split black gram dal. Make the idlis in the same way.

OR

You can pour one layer of batter, sprinkle leftover vegetables, or meat, and pour another layer of batter over it, and then steam the idlis. Serve with chutney or molagapudi (recipe pages 56-62/64).

RAVA IDLI

Semolina Rice Cakes

1 cup	fine semolina
2 tbsp	ghee
1" piece	ginger (grated)
3	green chillies (finely chopped)
¼ cup	chopped coriander leaves
½ cup	sour curd
	Salt to taste

Seasoning

2 tsp	ghee
1 tsp	mustard
1 tsp	cummin seeds
1 tbsp	ghee
2 tbsp	chopped cashew nuts

1. Fry the semolina in the ghee till pale gold in colour.

2. Add the ginger, green chillies, coriander leaves, sour curd and salt, using just enough water to make a thick batter.

3. Heat the ghee and season with mustard and cummin seeds and add to the batter.

4. Fry the cashew nuts in the ghee and add to the batter.

5. Mix all the ingredients well, and allow to ferment for an hour.

6. Make idlis in the usual way, and serve hot with coconut chutney (recipe page 56).

Makes 15 idlis

KANCHEEPURAM IDLI

Kancheepuram Rice Cakes

1 ½ cups	parboiled rice
1 cup	black gram dal
½ tsp	asafoetida
1 tsp	black pepper corns (pounded)
1 ½ tsp	ginger powder or fresh ground ginger
1 tsp	cummin seeds
	Salt to taste
¼ cup	oil
¼ cup	ghee
1 tsp	mustard seeds
10	curry leaves

1. Soak the rice and dal in water for 2-3 hours.

2. Grind the rice and dal coarsely to form a thick batter. Add the asafoetida, pepper, ginger, cummin seeds and salt. Allow to ferment for 24 hours till mixture becomes sour.

3. Heat the oil and ghee in a kadai and season with mustard seeds and curry leaves and add to batter.

4. Grease a pan large enough to hold the batter, and steam in a pressure cooker without the weight for 20 minutes.

5. Unmould the idli and cut into wedges and serve with any chutney.

Note: Do not use the perforated mould for making this idli.

Serves 4

ADUKKU IDLI

Sandwich Rice Cakes

This is a speciality among the Chettiars, and has many variations, and is a colourful dish. The chutneys may be substituted with masala vegetables, mince meat or chicken.

Basic idli batter as in recipe (page number 32)
4 tbsp	ghee
4 tbsp	grated coconut
	Oil for smearing idli moulds

1. Pour water into a vessel and place a colander which fits over it. An idli vessel is ideal if you have one. Take a piece of cloth large enough to fit into the colander, immerse in water and squeeze dry. Fit the cloth into the colander, pressing it against the sides and the bottom of the colander, so that the idli takes the shape.

2. Pour the batter into it to make an idli which is 8"in diameter and ¼" thick. Place the vessel on the stove, cover, and steam for about 10 minutes till the idli is cooked.

3. Gently ease it out of the colander, using a wet knife, and place on a serving plate and make the next one, and repeat once more, to make 3 large idlis.

4. Spread ghee on top of the first idli. Spread a generous amount of mint chutney (page 60). Place the second idli over it, spread ghee again, and spread tomato chutney. Sandwich with the third idli. Spread ghee over the third idli and sprinkle grated coconut over it. Cut idli into wedges and serve hot.

Serves 6

PANNIYARAM

Fried Rice-Lentil Cakes

3 cups	good quality raw rice
¾ cup	black gram dal
2 cups	oil

1. Soak the cleaned rice and dal for 30 minutes. Drain, and grind to a very smooth paste. Add salt to taste and mix well.

2. Heat 4 tablespoons of oil in a tawa. Drop spoonfuls of dough into the oil (the spoon should be deep not shallow). As the panniyarams cook and rise to the surface, splash the hot oil over them so that they are covered with oil as they cook. Flip each panniyaram over as it cooks. Remove from heat, drain on kitchen paper and serve hot with Daangar chutney (page 58).

Serves 5

ARISI PUTTU

Steamed Broken Rice

500 gm	good quality rice
1 cup	hot water
1 tsp	salt
3 tbsp	ghee
1 cup	sugar
1 cup	grated coconut

1. Clean the rice and soak for 15 minutes. Drain water, wash and spread the rice out on newspaper. After about half-an-hour, while the rice is till damp, grind the rice to powder. The powder should not be as smooth as in icing sugar, but coarser. It could be finer than the fine variety of semolina grains. Steam the flour for 10 minutes.

2. Remove from the stove, and mix it well with the finger tips, easing out any lumps that may be found. Sprinkle hot salt water, and steam again for 10 minutes. The rice puttu will have cooked and will be very soft.

3. Mix the ghee, sugar and grated coconut before serving.

Serves 7

SEMIYA UPPUMAV

Flavoured Vermicelli

500 gm vermicelli

Seasoning

½ cup	oil
2	cloves
2 (1" sticks)	cinnamon
2	cardamoms
1	onion (chopped)
6	green chillies (slit)
1	tomato (chopped)
1 tsp	ginger-garlic paste
3 + ½ cup	hot water
	Salt to taste

Garnish

½ cup	chopped coriander leaves

1. Broil the vermicelli in a kadai and set aside, but do not brown.

2. Heat oil in a kadai and season with cloves, cinnamon and cardamom.

3. Add onion and green chillies, and fry lightly till the onion is browned. Add tomato and ginger-garlic paste and fry for a few minutes.

4. Add 3 cups of hot water and salt. When the water boils, add the vermicelli, and stir till all the water is absorbed. If it is not cooked, sprinkle some hot water and cover with a lid.

5. Mix well before serving and garnish with chopped coriander leaves.

Serves 4-5

RAVA UPPUMAV

(Flavoured Semolina)

2 cups	semolina

Seasoning

½ cup	oil
1 tsp	mustard seeds
1 tsp	split black gram dal
1 tbsp	Bengal gram(soaked in water for 15 minutes)
5	red chillies(broken)
6	curry leaves
1	medium sized onion (sliced fine)
¾ tsp	ginger-garlic paste
½	lime
1 sprig	coriander leaves (chopped)

1. Clean and sift the semolina. Fry lightly in a kadai, stirring well, but do not brown. Transfer on to a plate.

2. Heat about 2½ cups of water, and keep it simmering on the stove.

3. Heat oil in the same kadai and season with mustard seeds, split black gram dal, Bengal gram dal, red chillies and curry leaves. Add onion slices, brown, and add ginger-garlic paste, fry lightly.

4. Add 2 cups of hot water, and salt to taste. When the water boils add the semolina, stirring vigorously to avoid lumps being formed. If the semolina is not cooked, sprinkle some of the hot water on to the mixture, taking care to add very small quantities at a time, otherwise the whole mixture will turn soggy. Squeeze the juice of the lime over the uppumav and mix well. Cover with a lid and leave on low heat.

5. Stir after a few minutes and sprinkle chopped coriander leaves.

Serves 5

VEN PONGAL

Savoury Lentil-Rice

2 cups	raw rice
1 cup	green gram dal
3 tbsp	ghee
2 tbsp	oil
1 tbsp	black pepper corns
1 tbsp	cummin seeds
¼ tsp	asoefatida powder
2	sprigs curry leaves
1 tsp	crushed ginger
	Salt to taste
3 tbsp	cashew nuts

1. Clean and wash the rice and dal. Drain the water.

2. Heat the oil and ghee in a pressure cooker, and season with pepper corns first, then cummin seeds and asoefatida and curry leaves. When the seasoning crackles, add ginger and fry for a minute.

3. Add the dal and fry for a couple of minutes.

4. Add 7 cups of water and salt to taste, and add the drained rice. Mix well and pressure cook for 5-7 minutes.

5. Brown the halved cashew nuts in a little ghee and spread over the pongal before serving.

6. Serve with coconut chutney and tamarind gravy (recipe on page 56, 220, 221).

Serves 6

POORI

Fried Indian Bread

4 cups	whole wheat flour
1 cup	refined flour
2 tbsp	curd
	Salt to taste
2 cups	oil for deep frying

1. Mix the two kinds of flour well, and add salt.

2. Add the curd, and knead together with cold water. The dough should be firm but pliable, and not soft as in chapatti dough.

3. Make lime sized smooth balls with the palms of the hands.

4. Sprinkle some rice flour on the rolling board and roll into thin rounds evenly.

5. Heat the oil till it is smoking hot, and immerse the in it fully. When the puffs up turn over and allow to cook.

6. Drain the s thoroughly and place them on paper to take off the excess oil.

Serve hot with potato puttu (recipe on page 237).

Serves 6

MASALA ROTI

Savoury Bread

1 loaf	bread
2 cups	chopped coriander leaves
6	green chillies
½ "	ginger
6	cloves garlic
4	black pepper corns
5	eggs
1 ½ cups	milk
½ tsp	turmeric powder
	Salt to taste
	Oil for frying bread

1. Slice the bread evenly, and arrange on a plate. The crust need not be used, and you should get about 15 slices.

2. Grind to a fine paste coriander leaves, chillies, ginger, garlic and pepper corns.

3. Beat the eggs with the milk, turmeric powder and salt. Blend the paste into the mixture.

4. Dip the bread slices in the egg mixture and fry on a tawa till golden brown.

Serve hot with tomato sauce.

Note: For strict vegetarians, this can be made without eggs. A tablespoon of cream may be added, with a heaped tablespoon of gram flour.

Serves 5

CHAPATTI

Griddle Fried Whole Wheat Indian Bread

2 cups	whole wheat flour
	Salt to taste
1 tbsp	oil
	Oil for frying

1. Mix the flour and the salt with the finger tips.

2. Make a well in the centre of the flour, add oil and mix again.

3. Using cold water, knead to make a soft pliable dough, cover and set aside for 2 hours.

4. Divide the dough into 8-10 portions and make each into a round smooth ball.

5. Roll out into rounds 5" in diameter. Pour half a teaspoon of oil in the centre and smear evenly. Sprinke flour. Fold in half and smear a little oil again. Sprinkle flour, then fold in half again so that it becomes a quarter of a circle. Prepare the entire dough this way.

6. Roll out the chappatis, keeping the triangular shape.

7. Place a tawa on medium heat, and place the rolled chappati on it. When slight bubbles appear on the surface, turn it over, and pour half a teaspoon of oil around it, and allow to cook on that side. Turn it over once more and press down with a soft cloth so that the heat is distributed evenly, and the other

side gets cooked as well. If the dough has been kneaded properly, the chapatti will puff up and will turn out very soft. Fry the rest of the chapattis the same way.

8. Line an airtight shallow container with soft cloth, place the cooked chapattis in it, cover with the cloth and seal with the lid.

Serve chapattis piping hot, with curries.

Makes 8-10 chapattis depending on the size required.

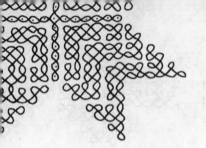

ULUNDU VADAI

Lentil Patties

2 cups	black gram dal
1 large	onion
8	green chillies
½ cup	coriander leaves
½"	ginger (grated)
1 tsp	ghee
	Salt to taste
3 cups	oil for frying

1. Soak the black gram in water for 2 hours, clean and drain.

2. Grind the dal without adding too much water. The batter should be finely ground, and thick enough to hold its shape when formed into vadais.

3. Chop onions, green chillies and coriander leaves fine. Add to batter along with the grated ginger, ghee and salt. Mix well.

4. Heat the oil in a kadai.

5. Grease a small banana leaf or a small square of thick plastic and place on a smooth firm surface, like an inverted plate.

6. Dip your hands in water and form a lime sized ball from the batter, and press it on the leaf or plastic to form an even round shape. Make a hole in the centre using your finger, and ease gently into the smoking hot oil.

7. Repeat the process till a batch of 5-6 vadais are frying in the kadai. Turn over each vadai, and fry as many as required.

Serve piping hot with mint or coconut chutney.

Makes about 35 vadais

THAYIR VADAI

Lentil Patties in Curd

15	vadais (as in recipe on page 46)
6 - 7cups	beaten curd
1tsp	mustard seeds
1tsp	split black gram dal
12	curry leaves
1 tbsp	oil
¼ cup	coriander leaves (chopped fine)

1. Place the vadais in a large shallow container while still hot, and pour the beaten curd over it.

2. Season with the mustard seeds, split black gram dal, and the curry leaves in 1 tablespoon of oil, and pour over the curd.

3. Chill in the refrigerator and garnish with coriander leaves before serving.

Serves 5

MASALA VADAI

Bengal Gram Patties

2 cups	Bengal gram
1	medium sized onion
5	green chillies
1	small bunch (¼ cup) dill (chopped)
1 tsp	ghee
½ tsp	baking powder
3 cloves	garlic
	Salt to taste
2 cups	oil for frying

1. Soak the gram for 2 hours.

2. Chop onion and green chillies finely. Clean and wash the dill and chop the leaves fine. Pound the garlic coarsely.

3. Clean and drain the gram, and coarsely grind in the mixie.

4. Add onion, chillies, dill, ghee, baking powder, garlic and salt and mix thoroughly.

5. Shape into lime sized balls, flatten with your fingers, and deep fry. Serve hot as a tea time snack.

Makes about 25 vadais

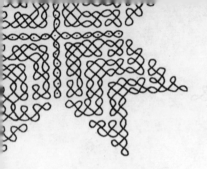

BONDA

Potato Balls

1 recipe	potato puttu, made dry (see page 237)
3 cups	gram flour
A pinch of	baking powder
	Salt to taste
2 cups	oil for frying

1. Make lime sized balls, using your hands to compress each ball, removing any moisture that may be present.

2. Make a thick batter with the gram flour, baking powder, salt and cold water.

3. Coat each ball with the batter and deep fry till golden brown.

Serve hot with coconut chutney.

Makes 30 balls

PAKODA

Onion-Lentil Fries

½ cup	Bengal gram flour
1 ½ cups	rice flour
1	medium sized onion
4	green chillies
¼ cup	chopped coriander leaves
A pinch of	asafoetida powder
2 tsp	ghee
¼ tsp	soda bicarbonate
	Salt to taste
2 cups	oil for frying

1. Mix the gram flour and rice flour with cold water to form a mixture which resembles breadcrumbs. Add a little more water to bind it.

2. Finely chop the onions and green chillies and add to the batter. Add coriander leaves, and asoefatida. Add the ghee, soda bicarbonate and salt, and mix well.

3. Drop small balls into hot oil and deep fry.

Makes about 30 pakodas

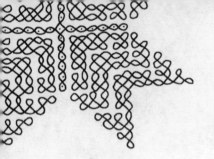

KHARA KOZHAKATTAI

Savoury Rice Flour Cakes

*This a speciality for Ganesh Chaturthi
and Varalakshmi puja.*

½ kg	raw rice flour
1 lt	water
½ tsp	salt
3 tbsp	oil

For the Filling

150 gm	Bengal gram dal
100 gm	black gram dal
8	green chillies (finely chopped)
1 bunch	coriander leaves (finely chopped)
½ tsp	pepper powder
¼ tsp	asafoetida powder
½	coconut(grated)
1	lime (juice extracted)
	Salt to taste

1. If you wish to make the flour at home consult recipe
    for Adhirasams (page 286). Sift the flour.

2. Boil the water with salt. Remove half the quantity

of water and store in another vessel. Add oil to the boiling water, keep it simmering, and add rice flour gradually, mixing vigorously. Once the water is used up sprinkle hot water which has been kept aside, on the dough, as much as is needed to make a soft dough. Set aside in another vessel and keep it covered with a moist cloth.

3. Pressure cook both the dals, and boil till the water is absorbed. Mash coarsely. Add the other ingredients listed below. Knead and set aside.

4. Pat a lime sized ball of dough into a circle, as thin as can be done without breaking, and place a teaspoonful of filling on one half of it. Moisten one half of the circle, fold over the other half and pinch the edges to seal it. Repeat the process till all the kozhakattais are done. Steam them in batches.

5. Brush with ghee before serving

Makes 20 Kozhakattais

CHUTNEYS

Chutneys, hot or mild, form a very important part of the Tamilian tiffin. A fried snack accompanied by a mild dip-like coconut chutney, is delicious. Pongal, uppumav, bondas, vadais, and the ubiquitous dosai or idli are never complete without the chutney to glorify it. Coconut based chutneys are most popular and can be prepared in a variety of ways.

Chutneys can be stored in the refrigerator, and on odd days when there has been very little time to cook, rice mixed with chutney and flavoured with a teaspoon of ghee can be a delicious main dish.

THENGAI THUVAIYAL

Coconut Chutney

½	coconut(grated)
5 small	green chillies
3 tbsp	fried gram dal
½" piece	ginger (chopped)
	Marble sized ball tamarind (remove seeds)
	Salt to taste

Seasoning

1 tbsp	oil
1 tsp	mustard seeds
1 tbsp	split black gram dal
8	curry leaves

1. Grind the coconut, green chillies, fried gram dal, ginger, tamarind and salt in a mixie.

2. Heat oil in a small pan and season with mustard seeds, split black gram dal and curry leaves. Pour over chutney, and mix well before serving. Add water if necessary.

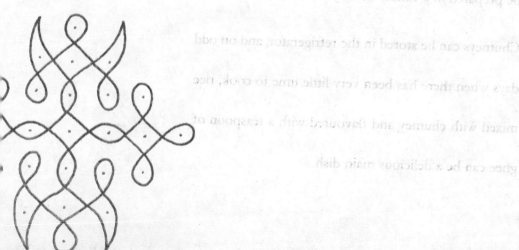

THAKKALI THUVAIYAL

Tomato chutney

2	onions
1" piece	ginger
5	red chillies
2 tbsp	oil
6 large	ripe tomatoes
	Salt to taste
1 tsp	mustard seeds
1 tsp	split black gram dal

1. Chop onions and ginger, and fry in 1 tablespoon of oil till onions turn brown.

2. Blanche tomatoes, remove skin and chop into small pieces.

3. Add to other ingredients, and fry for 3 minutes.

4. Add salt and grind to a paste in the mixie.

5. Heat the rest of the oil in a small pan and add mustard seeds and the dal. When it splutters, add the ground paste and fry on low heat for 5 minutes till the oil rises to the top.

Serve with hot dosais or chapattis.

DAANGAR CHUTNEY

Shallot Chutney

1 tbsp	oil
½ tsp	mustard seeds
½ tsp	split black gram dal
20	curry leaves
250 gm	shallots
1 pod	garlic
25	red chillies (broken into small pieces and deseeded)
1	lime sized ball tamarind
	Salt to taste

1. Heat the oil in a kadai and season with mustard seeds, black gram dal and curry leaves. Add the shallots, brown, and add garlic and chillies, and fry on low heat till the ingredients are well blended.

2. Add salt and extract from tamarind. Add half a cup of water and let it boil till it becomes thick. Serve hot.

GETTI CHUTNEY
Thick Lentil Chutney

3 heaped tbsp	Bengal gram
3 heaped tbsp	black gram dal
3 heaped tblsp	red chillies
1 dtsp	thick tamarind extract
½	fresh coconut (grated)
	Salt to taste

1. Broil dals to a golden brown colour and then the chillies.

2. Grind all the ingredients to a medium coarse thick paste.

Serve with hot rice and a dash of ghee for flavour.

VENGAYYA THUVAIYAL
Onion Chutney

3 tbsp	sesame oil
3	medium sized (50gm) onions
10	red chillies
2 tbsp	black gram dal
1 lime sized	tamarind ball
	Salt to taste

1. Chop onions and fry in 1 tablespoon oil till transparent. Set aside.

2. In the same pan fry red chillies and black gram dal in 1 tablespoon of oil.

3. Grind the roasted ingredient to a smooth paste with tamarind and salt.

4. Heat the remaining oil and fry the paste for 2-3 minutes.

This chutney can be preserved for 3 days in the refrigerator, and is an excellent accompaniment to dosais, pongal or chapattis.

PUDINA THUVAIYAL

Mint chutney

1 ½ cups	mint leaves
1 ½ cups	coriander leaves
1 tbsp	oil
1 tbsp	black gram dal
5	green chillies
1	marble sized ball tamarind
½" piece	ginger
1 cup	grated coconut
½ tsp	sugar
	Salt to taste

1. Wash the mint and coriander leaves, and squeeze out the water.

2. Heat the oil in a kadai and fry black gram dal first followed by green chillies, tamarind and ginger. Remove from heat and add the mint leaves and coriander leaves and stir well. If mint leaves are fried too much they will emit a bitter taste. Grind together all the ingredients with the grated coconut, salt and sugar.

THUVAIYAL

Garlic Chutney

½	coconut (grated)
6 cloves	garlic
4 tbsp	fried gram dal
	Salt to taste

Grind all the ingredients together and serve with dosais or idlis. This bland chutney makes an excellent accompaniment for tamarind curries (page 220-224), especially pepper curry (page 222).

KATHRIKKAI THUVAIYIL

Brinjal Chutney

1 tbsp	oil
6	red chillies
¼ tsp	asafoetida powder
250 gm	brinjals
12	shallots
2 large	tomatoes
3 tbsp	grated coconut
1	marble sized ball tamarind
	Salt to taste

1. Heat oil in a pan and fry the red chillies and asafoetida. Remove and set aside.

2. Roast the brinjal, remove skin and chop into pieces.

3. Chop the shallots and tomatoes.

4. In the same pan heat the oil left behind, and fry the brinjal, shallots and tomatoes.

5. Grind these fried ingredients with coconut, tamarind and salt.

6. Add the seasoning and grind for a minute longer.

May be served with idlis, dosais or ven pongal.

CARROT THUVAIYAL

Carrot Chutney

1 tbsp	oil
1 tsp	vadagam OR
½ tsp	mustard
½ tsp	cummin seeds
½ tsp	split black gram dal
¼ tsp	fenugreek seeds
200gm	carrots
1	marble sized ball tamarind
½" piece	ginger
10	curry leaves
2 tbsp	chopped coriander leaves
4	red chillies
	Salt to taste

1. Heat the oil, and season with vadagam, or the 4 ingredients listed below it.

2. Grate the carrots, and add to the seasoning, and fry till it becomes limp.

3. Add the remaining ingredients, and fry for 5 minutes on low heat.

4. Cool, add salt, and grind to paste in a mixie.

PODIS

Flavoured Powders

The *podis* or hot spicy powders are part of the 'ready mix' food so part of Tamilian culture, and are common to Andhra and Karnataka. Prepared in a variety of ways, the *podis* can be eaten with hot rice and ghee, some of them blended into curries, each with its own distinctive flavour. Some *podis,* like the curry leaf *podi,* guarantees easy digestion, and it is believed that curry leaves, consumed regularly wards off premature grey hair! Some guarantee running eyes and nose with their pungency, with such lip smacking flavours that they are difficult to resist!

MOLAGAPODI

Chilli Flavoured Powder

1 cup	Bengal gram
1 cup	black gram dal
3 tbsp	sesame seeds
1 tsp	asafoetida
1 ½ cups	red chillies
1 tbsp	oil
1	marble sized ball tamarind
	Salt to taste

1. Broil the dals, sesame seeds and asafoetida till golden brown.

2. Fry the red chillies in the oil.

3. Add tamarind and salt and grind coarsely. Cool and store in airtight bottles.

An ideal accompaniment for idlis and dosais. Place a small mound of molagapodi next to the idlis or dosais, and make a little well in the centre with your finger. Pour a teaspoon of pure gingelly oil into the well, and mix the oil with the powder. This is a delicious crunchy spicy dip for idlis and dosais.

YELLU PODI

Sesame Flavoured Powder

1 cup	black sesame seeds
5	garlic pods (unskinned)
6	red chillies
	Salt to taste

1. Broil sesame seeds, garlic and red chillies till the sesame seeds crackle.

2. Remove immediately from heat, add salt and then make into a powder.

Serve with idlis.

CURRYVEPPILLAI PODI

Curry Leaf Powder

2 tbsp	oil
3 cups	curry leaves
2 tbsp	black pepper corns
1 tsp	cummin seeds
2 tbsp	black gram dal
1	marble sized ball tamarind
	Salt to taste

1. Fry curry leaves in oil till crisp.
2. Broil the rest of the ingredients except salt.
3. Powder medium coarse, mix salt, cool and store in airtight bottles.

Serve with hot rice and ghee.

Note: *In my family, whenever a woman delivered a baby, curry leaf powder was part of her daily diet, for 10 days! Denied all spices during the lactation period, I remember how eagerly we looked forward to this concession of pepper in a hot podi.*

SAMBHAR PODI

Powder for Lentil Curry

Sambhar powder is added to enhance the taste of sambhar.

2 cups	coriander seeds
2 cups	red chillies
½ cup	Bengal gram
4 tbsp	cummin seeds
4 tbsp	pepper corn
1 ½ tsp	mustard seeds
1 ½ cup	curry leaves
1" piece	cinnamon
3	cloves
2 tsp	turmeric powder

Broil each ingredient separately, till crisp, except the turmeric powder. Grind finely, cool and store in airtight containers.

RASAM PODI

Powder for Lentil Soup

Rasam powder is added to the rasam after it is taken off the fire.

1 cup	red chillies
1 tbsp	oil
1 cup	black pepper corns
1 cup	cummin seeds
¾ cup	coriander seeds
1 cup	red gram dal
¾ cup	black gram dal
¾ cup	Bengal gram dal
½ cup	fenugreek seeds
2 cups	curry leaves
6	pea sized pieces asafoetida

Fry the asafoetida pieces evenly in the oil, taking care not to burn them. Broil each of the ingredients separately on low heat, and powder fine collectively in a mixie. Store in an airtight container.

Note: *For a small family, or in homes where rasam is not made daily, the recipe may be halved or quartered.*

VADAGAM

Seasoning Mixture

*V*adagams are preserved seasonings used for sambars, tamarind and fish gravies, and some non-vegetarian curries. They enhance the existing flavours of the curries, and the intriguing aroma is irresistible. The process may seem somewhat complicated, but with the present day gadgets, the whole pattern has been simplified. It is advisable to try make the vadagams only in bright sunny weather, but I know some enterprising young women living in cold countries who have resorted to warm ovens to subsitute for the sun, much to the consternation of die hard traditionalists who swear that it just isn't the same...

1 kg	shallots or sambhar onions
¼ kg	garlic
2 cups	curry leaves
1 cup	mustard seeds
1 cup	red dal
1 cup	black gram dal
1 cup	cummin seeds
½ cup	fenugreek seeds
½ cup	gingelly oil (used only for dipping)
2 tbsp	castor oil

1. Grind onions coarsely and retain liquid.

2. Separate garlic flakes and grind coarsely, with the skin.

3. Grind curry leaves coarsely.

4. Using a wide deep vessel, thoroughly mix onions, garlic and curry leaves and add the mustard seeds, red gram dal, black gram dal, cummin seeds, and fenugreek seeds one ingredient at a time, mixing well after each addition. Cover the utensil with a lid and allow the ingredients to soak overnight.

5. In the morning take a handful of the mixture, squeeze out the liquid into the vessel, and form tightly into a ball as large as your hands can hold. Repeat the process till all the ingredients are used. Arrange the balls on a big tray and place directly in the sunlight till sunset.

6. Crumble the balls and add to the liquid, the last thing at night, allowing it to soak through till the next morning.

7. Repeat process every morning and night, till all the liquid is absorbed.

8. Crumble the balls for the last time, add 2 table-spoons castor oil and form into balls and dry in the sun. Each morning before placing the balls in the sun, smear your hands generously with gingelly oil, and compress the balls in the hollows of your hands, retaining the perfect spherical shape at the same time forcing the moisture to be expelled to the surface.

9. The process is repeated till the vadagams are bone dry.

Store in air tight containers to last for a year or more depending how effective they are sun dried.

The process may take about two weeks, and it makes about 24 balls.

RICE DISHES & PULAOS

The Tamilian loves his rice and feels cheated if he does not have a fair helping of it. A variety of rice is available in the granaries of the South, and Tanjore is known as the rice bowl of India. White rice is cooked every day at least for lunch and eaten with curries, rasam or curds. Most people cook raw rice, but health freaks prefer hand pounded non-milled rice. Some communities prefer to eat parboiled rice which is certainly more healthful.

On special occasions, rice is used for an exotic dish like a pulao both vegetarian and non-vegetarian and is always taken with a raw salad. Pulaos are also made with vermicelli or semolina and a pulao is a meal-in-one.

KARI PULAO

Mutton Pulao

500 gms	mutton
3 cups	Basmati rice
3 large	onions
3	green chillies
1 small spring	mint leaves

Grind to a fine paste

5	cloves
5 (1" pieces)	cinnamon
5	cardamoms
3 pods	garlic
2 ½" piece	ginger
10	red chillies

Seasoning

¾ cup	oil
¼ cup	ghee
2	bay leaves
2 tsp	turmeric powder
1 cup	curd
	Salt to taste

To Garnish

2 tbsp	oil
3 large	onions
250 gm	peas
½ cup	chopped coriander leaves

1. Clean the mutton and cut into large pieces.

2. Clean and wash the rice and soak in water.

3. Slice the onions lengthwise, and slit the green chillies. Remove leaves from mint sprig, wash, and set aside.

4. Clean the garlic removing outer skin. Scrape the

ginger and clean thoroughly, before grinding the listed ingredients to a fine paste.

5. Heat the oil and ghee in the pressure cooker, and add the bay leaves.

6. Add onions and green chillies and fry till onions turn golden brown. Add the mint leaves. Add the ground masala and fry on low heat till the oil rises to the top. Add meat and turmeric powder and fry for 5 to 7 minutes. Beat the curds and pour over the meat. Add enough salt for the meat, and add just enough water to cook the meat, between 2 to 3 cups.

7. Pressure cook for 10 to 15 minutes till meat is fairly well done but should not be too tender.

8. While the meat is cooking, prepare the garnish. Slice onions finely lengthwise, and fry in oil till dark brown. Cook peas with salt till tender.

9. Remove cooked meat from gravy. Measure the gravy and top with enough water so that the liquid is double the quantity of rice, in this case 6 cups. Taste the liquid and if salt is less add required amount. Add the juice of one lime.

10. Heat the gravy and when it begins to boil, add the rice. This may be done in a pressure cooker for 3 minutes after the pressure hiss, or in a rice cooker. Do not open till serving time.

11. Garnish with boiled peas, chopped coriander and browned onions.

Serve hot with tomato or cucumber pachidi (recipe page 102 & 104) and Yenna Kathrikkai Curry (recipe page 218).

Serves 5

Note: *Pulao prepared without any ghee (only oil) is equally tasty.*

KOZHI PULAO

Chicken Pulao

2 small	chicken (750-800gm each)
1 kg	Basmati rice
1 large	coconut

Grind to a paste

2	cloves
½" piece	cinnamon
1 large	onion
2" piece	ginger
2 pods	garlic (about 45 flakes)
12	green chillies
1	large bunch coriander leaves
6	mint leaves
1 tbsp	coriander seeds

Seasoning

4 tbsp	oil or ghee
2	bay leaves
4	cloves
4	cardamoms
3 (1" pieces)	cinnamon
4 large	onions(sliced lengthwise)
½ cup	curd
2 tsp	turmeric powder
1	lime

1. Remove the skin from the chicken, clean and cut into large pieces.

2. Clean and wash the rice and soak in water.

3. Grate the coconut and extract 1 ½ cups thick milk and 1 cup thin milk.

74

4. Grind the masala, blend with curd, and coat the chicken pieces with the paste.

5. Cook the rice, straining it before it is fully cooked. Drain in a wide colander, and after the moisture has completely drained, spread out on a large plate, and add salt, mixing it in evenly.

6. Heat the oil or ghee in a heavy vessel, and temper with the bay leaves and the whole spices. Add the onions, and when transparent, add the chicken with the masala and the turmeric powder. Fry till oil rises to the top, add the thin coconut milk and salt just enough for the chicken and cook chicken till nearly done. Take care not to overcook the chicken, as this will reduce it to fibre since more cooking is entailed.

7. Pour in the thick coconut milk and boil till the gravy is thick and the chicken tender. Add the juice of the lime. Pour the gravy into another bowl, and allow to settle. Pour off the surface oil into a cup.

8. Spoon a little bit of the oil into the same heavy vessel and pour some of the chicken gravy, spreading it evenly. Layer it with part of the rice. Repeat the process with alternate layers of gravy and rice till both are used up. Pour the remaining oil/ghee right on top and cover with a well fitting lid. Cook on very low heat. Occasionally stir the pulao with a long flat ladle. If the moisture is used up and the rice is not cooked, sprinkle a little hot water, and cook till the rice is soft.

Serve hot with curd based pachidi (recipe pages 102-105).

Serves 7

ELLUMICHAPAZHAM SADAM

Lime Rice

3 cups	rice
	salt to taste
2 ½	limes
1 tbsp	Bengal gram dal

Seasoning

1 ½ tbsp	oil
1 tsp	mustard seeds
2 tbsp	fried peanuts (with skin removed)
1 tsp	split black gram dal
8	curry leaves
4	red chillies (each broken in two)
1 tsp	turmeric powder
2 tbsp	water

1. Wash and clean the rice and cook it in such a way that each grain is separate. The best method is boiling the rice and straining it till all the water is removed. Extract juice from limes, and blend the rice with lime juice and salt. Set aside.

2. Soak the Bengal gram dal for half an hour.

3. Heat the oil in a heavy kadai, and season with mustard seeds, halved peanuts, split black gram dal, curry leaves and red chillies. Add turmeric powder and water and sauté till the raw smell of turmeric disappears.

4. Add the rice and blend the whole evenly with a flat spoon, gently, so that the rice is not broken or over-cooked. If the lime rice is not sour enough, squeeze more lime into it and mix thoroughly.

Serves 5

Rice forms an essential part of Tamilian cuisine.
Here is Kozhi Pulao (Chicken Pulao) with a salad.

1. Kozhi Pulao (Chicken Pulao)
2. Pachidi (Salad)

*The traditional and heavy grinding stones are often replaced
now by modern mixies though many cooks claim the
authentic flavour can only be obtained the traditional way.*

1. Grinding stone for powdering ingredients
2. Grinding stone for masala
3. Lentils
4. Rice
5. Pepper Corns

VENDHIKEERAI SADAM

Green Fenugreek Rice

3 cups	Basmati rice
5 small bunches	fenugreek leaves
2	onions
6	green chillies

Seasoning

2 tbsp	oil
1 tbsp	ghee
4	cloves
2 (1" pieces)	cinnamon
3	cardamom
12	cashew nuts
2 tsp	ginger-garlic paste
	Salt to taste

1. Wash rice and soak in water.

2. Remove fenugreek leaves from stems, wash thoroughly and chop fine.

3. Slice onions lengthwise and slit green chillies.

4. Heat ghee and oil in a pressure cooker, season with whole spices. Add onions and green chillies and when onions are transparent, add the chopped fenugreek leaves and fry for 5 minutes.

5. Add slit cashew nuts and fry lightly, then add the ginger-garlic paste. Add 6 cups of water and salt to taste.

6. Drain the rice, add to liquid, and pressure cook for 3 minutes.

Serve hot with tomato pachidi (recipe page 102) and meat ball curry (recipe page 137).

Serves 5

YERRA PULAO

Prawn Pulao

500 gm	prawns
3 cups	rice

Grind to a paste

7	red chillies
3	cloves
3	cardamoms
1 ½" piece	cinnamon
1 full pod	garlic
2" piece	ginger
2	tomatoes
1 tsp	turmeric powder

Seasoning

¾ cup	ghee and/or oil
1	bay leaf
3	medium sized onions (sliced)
	Salt to taste

To Garnish

½ cup	chopped coriander leaves

1. Shell prawns, devein, clean and set aside.

2. Wash rice, and cook till nearly done. Drain the water, and spread the rice on a large plate.

3. Heat oil/ghee in a pan, and add bay leaf.

Add onions and fry till brown. Add the ground masala and fry for a couple of minutes. Add the prawns and salt and sauté till they are cooked. Add a little extra salt for the rice.

4. Place a layer of prawn masala gravy in a heavy vessel, and spread a layer of rice. Alternate the gravy and rice till they are both used up. Close with a well fitting lid and cook on low heat. After 5-8 minutes check whether the rice is fully cooked and if the liquid has been absorbed fully. If it has and the rice needs to be done further, pour a little hot water evenly around the rice. Mix gently till the masala gets distributed.

Serve with tomato pachidi (recipe page 102).

Serves 6

THENGAI SADAM

Coconut Rice

½ kg	Basmati rice
1	large coconut

Seasoning

½ cup	ghee or oil
3	bay leaves
3	cloves
2	cardamoms
2 (1" pieces)	cinnamon
12	cashew nuts (halved)
2	onions
6	green chillies
2 tsp	ginger-garlic paste
¼ tsp	turmeric powder
5	mint leaves
1	lime (juice extracted)
	Salt to taste

To Garnish

200 gms	fresh green peas (boiled)
½ cup	chopped coriander

1. Measure the rice with a cup, wash and clean it and soak in water.

2. Grate the coconut, and extract milk adding water to make the volume of liquid double that of the rice.

3. Heat the ghee or oil in a pressure cooker, and add bay leaves and whole spices, and cashew nuts last. When the cashew nuts turn light brown, add onions and green chillies and fry till onions turn light brown.Add ginger garlic paste and turmeric powder and sauté for a minute and them add mint leaves.

4. Add the coconut milk, salt and lime juice.

5. Add the rice, and pressure cook for two minutes. Switch off heat and allow the cooker to cool to room temparature,

6. Before serving, garnish the coconut rice with boiled peas and chopped coriander leaves.

Serve hot with chicken curry (recipe page162) and tomato pachidi (recipe page102).

Serves 5

KAIKARI PULAO

Vegetable Pulao

2 cups	Basmati rice
½ kg	mixed vegetables (cauliflower, carrots, beans and/peas)
3	onions

Grind to a paste

4	cloves
1 ½"	cinnamon stick
4	cardamoms
4	green chillies
½ tsp	chilli powder
2 tsp	coriander powder
1 ½" piece	ginger
10 flakes	garlic
1 tsp	fennel seeds
2 tsp	poppy seeds
1 tsp	turmeric powder

Seasoning

5 tbsp	ghee or oil or mixture of both
1	bay leaf
2 tbsp	mint leaves
3 tbsp	chopped coriander leaves
	Salt to taste

To Garnish

3	boiled eggs, halved (optional)
2 tbsp	halved cashew nuts (fried)
½ cup	chopped coriander leaves

1. Clean and wash the rice and allow to soak.

2. Dice the vegetables, and slice the onions.

3. Grind the listed ingredients to a fine paste.

4. Heat the oil/ghee in a pressure cooker, and season with bay leaves. Add onions and fry to a light brown. Add the ground masala and fry for a few minutes on low heat. Add mint and coriander leaves.

5. Pour 4 cups of water, mix well and add salt to taste. Add the drained rice, and vegetables. Pressure cook for 4-5 minutes.

Garnish with the boiled eggs, chopped coriander leaves and sprinkle fried cashew nuts on the surface.

Serve hot with any pachidi (recipe pages 102-105) and egg curry (recipe page 196).

Serves 5

KATHRIKKAI SADAM

Brinjal Rice

½ kg	Basmati rice
½ kg	brinjals (long white variety)
½	coconut (grated)

Seasoning

1 cup	ghee and oil (in any proportion desired)
2 large	bay leaves
1 piece	cinnamon
2	cloves
2	cardamoms
4	onions (cut lengthwise)
3	green chillies (slit lengthwise)
½ tsp	turmeric powder
3 tsp	ginger garlic paste
3	medium sized tomatoes (chopped)
½ cup	thick curd
1	lime
	Salt to taste

Grind to a paste

6	green chillies
1 cup	coriander leaves (chopped)
3	cloves
2	cinnamon
2	cardamoms
¼ tsp	fennel seeds
1 tsp	roasted coriander seeds
1 tsp	poppy seeds

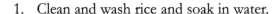

To Garnish

| ½ cup | chopped coriander |
| A handful of | cashew nuts |

1. Clean and wash rice and soak in water.

2. Wash brinjals, slit in 4 lengthwise three quarters of the way, keeping the stems intact.

3. Extract milk completely from grated coconut.

4. Heat oil or/and ghee in a pressure cooker, add bay leaves and whole spices. Add onions and green chillies, sauté till onions are transparent. Add turmeric powder, ginger-garlic paste and tomatoes, sauté for a few minutes. Add the curd and the ground masala, and sauté for a few minutes.

5. Add brinjals and salt and fry on low heat till brinjals become soft and half cooked.

6. Add the juice of the lime. Add coconut milk topped with water to make up a little less than twice the volume of rice used(for 3 cups of rice, you can add 2 ¾ cups of total liquid). Taste the liquid and add salt if necessary.

7. Pressure cook for 3 minutes. Do not open for at least three quarters of an hour till pressure is fully released.

8. Garnish with chopped coriander leaves and fried cashew nuts.

Serve hot with onion pachidi (recipe page 104).

Serves 5

THAKKALI SADAM

Tomato Rice

4 cups	Basmati rice
200-250 gms	paneer
2 tbsp	oil
4 large	tomatoes

Seasoning

3 tbsp	oil
1 tbsp	ghee
2	bay leaves
3 (1" pieces)	cinnamon
3	cardamoms
4	cloves
5	black peppercorns
2 large	onions (sliced lengthwise)
6	green chillies (slit)
3 tsp	ginger garlic paste
1 tsp	turmeric powder
	Salt to taste

To Garnish

2 large	onions (sliced fine lengthwise)
1 small bunch	coriander leaves

1. Wash rice and soak in water, for an hour.

2. Cut paneer into cubes and shallow fry in oil to a golden colour.

3. Blanch tomatoes, remove skin and liquidise in a mixie.

4. Cook rice till nearly done, strain and spread out on plate.

5. Heat ghee and oil in a heavy vessel and add bay leaves, followed by whole spices and pepper corns. Add onions and green chillies and sauté till the onions turn light brown. Add ginger garlic paste and turmeric powder and sauté for a few minutes.Add the tomato pureé and enough salt for the rice and sauté for 5 minutes. Add 1 cup of water and simmer for a few minutes till the raw smell of the tomato disappears.

6. Add the rice and close with a tight fitting lid letting the mixture simmer on very low heat. Gently stir now and then till water is completely absorbed and rice is cooked. If not cooked a little hot water may be sprinkled and the vessel kept on low heat till water is absorbed.

7. Fry the sliced onions till crisp and golden brown, and garnish with chopped coriander leaves, brown fried sliced onions onions and paneer.

Paneer can be substitued by green peas if one prefers.

Serve hot with kurma or any vegetarian or non-vegetarian curries of your choice and onion pachidi (see recipe on page 104).

Serves 5

RAVA PULAO

Semolina Pulao

3 cups	semolina
200 gm	green peas
250 gm	minced meat*
1 tsp	ginger-garlic paste
½ tsp	chilli powder
1 tsp	coriander powder
1 tsp	turmeric powder
	Salt to taste

Seasoning

¾ cup	oil
3	cloves
3	cardamoms
1 ½" piece	cinnamon
2	onions (chop fine)
6	green chillies (slit)
1 tsp	ginger-garlic paste
1 large	tomato
3 ½ cups	water (kept simmering on the stove)
1	lime (juice extracted)

To Garnish

½ cup	chopped coriander leaves

1. Clean the semolina, and broil in a kadai, but do not brown.

2. Boil the peas with a little salt and set aside.

3. Wash the minced meat and cook with ginger-garlic paste, chilli coriander powder, turmeric powder, and

salt to taste. Strain the broth and measure it.

4. In a heavy vessel, heat oil and add whole spices. After a couple of minutes, add the onions and green chillies. When the onions brown slightly, add ginger-garlic paste and tomatoes, and fry for a minute.

5. Add water to the meat broth to make 3 cups of liquid, and pour this into the vessel. When it boils, add the semolina and mince meat and the boiled green peas, stirring continously so that no lumps are formed.

6. If the semolina is not cooked, ladle a little hot water on to the pulao, taking care to add very little at a time. Too much water will make the pulao soggy. Cover with a lid, and keep on low heat for a few minutes.

7. Add lime juice, and garnish with chopped coriander leaves and boiled peas.

Serves 6

* Mince meat may be substituted with 2 cups of cubed vegetables like carrots, beans, potatoes, peas etc.

SEMIYA PULAO

Vermicelli Pulao

500 gm	vermicelli
250 gm	mixed vegetables (carrots, beans, peas and/or cauliflower)
½ tsp	ginger-garlic paste
½ tsp	chilli powder
1 tsp	coriander powder
½ tsp	turmeric powder
	Salt to taste

Seasoning

½	cup oil
2 tbsp	ghee
2	cloves
2 (1" pieces)	cinnamon
2	onions (sliced fine)
6	green chillies (slit)
1 tsp	ginger-garlic paste
2	tomatoes (chopped)
3+½ cup	water
	Salt to taste
1	lime

To Garnish

½ cup	chopped coriander leaves

1. Roast the vermicelli but do not allow it to brown.

2. Dice the vegetables, and cook with ½ teaspoon ginger-garlic paste, chilli, coriander and turmeric powder, and salt to taste. Keep on the stove till all

the water has been absorbed.

3. Heat oil in a heavy vessel, and season with whole spices. Add onions and green chillies, and fry lightly till the onion is browned. Add ginger-garlic paste and tomatoes, and fry for a few minutes.

4. Add 3 cups of hot water and salt. When the water boils, add the vermicelli and stir. Add the cooked vegetables after a few minutes and stir till all the water is absorbed.

5. If the vermicelli is still not cooked after the water is absorbed, sprinkle some hot water and stir. Add the lime juice, mixing it evenly.

6. Switch off the heat, garnish with chopped coriander and serve hot.

93

Serves 5-6

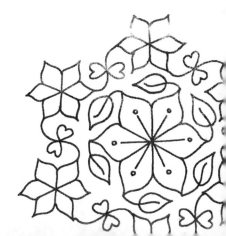

PULIYODORAI

Tamarind Rice

3 cups	rice
100 gms	tamarind

Roast and Powder

16	red chillies
2 tbsp	coriander seeds
1 tsp	sesame seeds
1 tsp	cummin seeds

Seasoning

½ cup	sesame oil
1 tsp	mustard seeds
1 tsp	split black gram dal
¼ tsp	asafoetida powder
8	red chillies (each broken in two)
1 tbsp	fried peanuts (skinned)
10	curry leaves
	Salt to taste

1. Clean and wash the rice and cook it till it is just done. Each grain should be separate. Spread out on a large plate and allow to cool.

2. Extract the juice from the tamarind. It should be thick.

3. Roast and powder the listed spices.

4. Heat oil in a pan and add mustard, split black gram dal. When it splutters, add 8 red chillies and add halved peanuts and curry leaves.

5. Fry for a couple of minutes, and tamarind juice and salt to taste and let it simmer till the oil rises to the top. Add the powdered spices, and mix well. Remove from heat.

6. Spoon the mixture on to the rice, mixing well after each addition. Add as much as desired. If the preference is for less spice, the mixture can be refrigerated in a bottle for further use. It can be heated, and mixed with leftover rice.

Serves 7-8

KARA SADAM

Hot Spicy Rice

My mother used to make this with leftover rice, and we called it kara (spicy hot) sadam. I remember how we loved it, and a favourite though not conventional combination was eating this with boiled eggs.

3 cups	cooked rice
	Salt to taste

Seasoning

3 tblsp	sesame oil
½ " piece	cinnamon
2	cloves
10	curry leaves
1	onion(chopped fine)
1 ½ tsp	chilli powder
2 tsp	coriander powder
1 tsp	turmeric powder
1	marble sized ball tamarind

1. Spread the cooked rice on a big plate and apply salt evenly.

2. Heat oil in a kadai, and add whole spices and curry leaves. Add chopped onion, and let it brown lightly. Add chilli and coriander powder, turmeric powder and tamarind extract. Simmer on low heat till oil rises to the top.

3. Add the cooked rice and stir till the spices are well mixed.

Serve hot.

Serves 8

THAYIR SADAM

Curd Rice

2 cups	rice
3 ½-4 cups	sour curd
	Salt to taste
½" piece	ginger (grated fine)
5	green chillies (chopped fine)

Seasoning

2 tbsp	oil
1 tsp	mustard seeds
1 tsp	split black gram dal
1 pea-sized	piece of asafoetida OR
A pinch of	asafoetida powder

To Garnish

½ small	carrot
¼ cup	chopped coriander leaves

1. Clean and wash the rice and slightly overcook. Mash while still hot and set aside, and allow to cool. Beat the curd lightly, add salt and blend with the rice. If mixture is too dry, add more curd, or some milk. Add the ginger and green chillies to the rice.

2. Heat the oil and season with mustard seeds, split black gram dal, curry leaves and asafoetida. Pour over the curd rice, mix in well, and refrigerate the rice.

3. Cut the carrot into delicate fine strips and soak in ice water till ready to be used. Just before serving, garnish the curd rice with coriander leaves and carrot strips.

Serve cold with hot mango pickle (recipe page 266).

Serves 6

KOOTAN CHORU

Lentil-Vegetable Rice Dish

A typical Vellala dish, this meal-in-one nutritious rice dish goes back three generations!

¾ cup	red gram dal
3	medium sized onions (siced thinly)
3 small	tomatoes
¼ tsp	turmeric powder
¼ tsp	asafoetida
	Salt to taste
2	medium sized (150 gm) brinjals
1	raw plantain
2	medium sized potatoes
2	drumsticks
¼ tsp	turmeric powder
1 ½ tsp	chilli powder
2 cups	rice

Seasoning

¾ cup	oil
¼ cup	ghee
1 ½ tsp	mustard seeds
1 ½ tsp	split black gram dal
10	curry leaves
1 bunch	drumstick leaves

1. Pressure cook the dal with the 5 ingredients listed below it.

2. Dice the brinjals, raw plantain and potatoes. Chop the drumsticks into 3" pieces. Cook the vegetables with turmeric powder, chilli powder and salt to taste. Add the drumsticks last, as they cook very fast.

3. Strain the dal and cooked vegetables, and set the liquid aside.

4. Measure the liquid and supplement with water to make it double the quantity of rice, in this case 4 cups. Wash and clean the rice and pressure cook the rice in this liquid. Add the dal and vegetables, and keep on heat till water is absorbed.

5. Heat ghee and oil in a heavy vessel and season with mustard seeds, split black gram (urad) dal, curry leaves and drumstick leaves. When it crackles, pour the seasoning into the rice dal mixture, mix well, and retain heat till the whole is well blended. Serve hot.

Serves 6

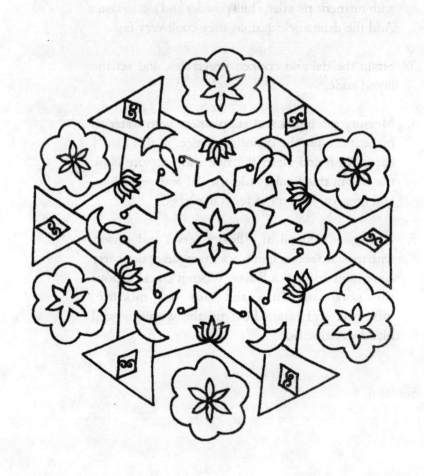

PACHIDI

Salads

Akin to the north Indian raithas which are curd based, the pachidi is a perfect complement to a hot biriyani or pulao tempering its exotic spicy taste with its gentle mix of curd and raw vegetables, delicious when it is cooled in the refrigerator.

THAKALLI PACHIDI

Tomato Salad

1 cup	chopped onions
1 cup	chopped tomatoes
3	green chillies
2 tbsp	chopped coriander leaves
½ tsp	sugar
	Salt to taste
2 ½ cups	curd

1. Chop the onions, tomatoes, green chillies very fine. Mix with coriander leaves, sugar and salt.

2. Beat the curd smooth, and pour over the chopped ingredients, mix well and refrigerate.

Serves 5

VELLRIKKAI PACHIDI

Cucumber Salad

½ kg	cucumber
6	green chillies
	Salt to taste
2	cups curd

Seasoning

2 tsp	oil
1 tsp	mustard seeds
1 tsp	split black gram dal
6	curry leaves

1. Slice each end of the cucumber, and rub on the cut edge to remove bitter taste. Pare the skin, and grate the cucumber fine. Mix with salt and set aside for 15 minutes.

2. Chop green chillies fine.

3. Squeeze out the water from the cucumber and add to green chillies.

4. Beat the curd till blended and pour over the salad.

5. Heat oil, season with the listed 3 ingredients and add to salad.

6. Mix lightly and chill in the refrigerator.

Serves 6

VENGAYYA PACHIDI

Onion Salad

4 large	onions (sliced finely)
6	green chillies
2 tbsp	grated coconut
2 cups	curd
	Salt to taste

1. Slice onions finely.

2. Slit 4 green chillies and add to the onions.

3. Grind remaining 2 chillies and coconut to a fine paste, and beat it with curd and salt.

4. Pour the curd mixture over the onions and chillies. Mix well and refrigerate till the meal is served.

Serves 6

PUDINA PACHIDI

Mint Salad

To Grind

½ cup	mint leaves
½ cup	coriander leaves
4	green chillies
1 tsp	black gram dal
1	marble sized ball tamarind
½ cup	grated coconut
3 cups	curd
2	onions
2	green chillies
	Salt to taste

1. Grind the first 6 listed ingredients to a fine paste.

2. Beat the curd lightly till smooth.

3. Slice onions and slit green chillies, and add to curd with salt. Add the ground paste, and mix the whole thoroughly.

Serves 6

VELANGAI PACHIDI

Wood Apple Salad

1	large wood apple
	Jaggery (measured to equal quantity of wood apple)
⅛ tsp	salt
1 tsp	oil
½ tsp	mustard
2	green chillies

1. Break open the wood apple, and scoop out the fleshy portion.

2. Measure this and add to it an equal quantity of jaggery, and salt. Mix well and add 3 tablespoons of water or more to enable even blending.

3. Heat the oil and season with mustard seeds and green chillies.

    Pour over the salad and mix.

Serves 5

MANGAI PACHIDI

Mango Salad

1	mango, not too tender or over-ripe
¾ cup	water
$1/_8$ tsp	turmeric powder
½ tsp	salt
90 gms	jaggery
2 tsp	rice flour

Seasoning

2 tsp	oil
1 tsp	mustard
2	green chillies

1. Cut the mango into large pieces. Remove the skin only if it is too thick.

2. Heat the water in a heavy vessel, and add the mango pieces, turmeric powder and salt, and let it cook till the mango is soft. Add jaggery and stir.

3. Blend the rice flour in a little water and add to mixture. Cook for a few minutes till the ingredients are well blended and remove from heat.

4. Heat the oil, season with mustard seeds and green chillies and add to the salad.

Serves 5

VEPPAI POO PACHIDI

Neem Flower Salad

This salad is supposed to be auspicious for Tamil New Year day, and is prepared with fresh neem flowers.

2 tsp	petals of neem flowers
2 tsp	oil

Seasoning

4 tsp	oil
1 tsp	mustard seeds
6	red chillies
1	pea sized piece of asafoetida
4	curry leaves
1	lime sized ball tamarind
	Salt to taste
1 dsp	jaggery
2 tsp	rice flour

1. Pluck the petals of the neem flower, clean and fry in 2 teaspoons of oil to a dark red colour, and then powder.

2. Heat the oil, and add mustard, broken red chillies, asafoetida and curry leaves, sautéing till the seasoning crackles.

3. Extract tamarind juice making up 1 cup of liquid, and add to the above mixture. Add salt and boil for 2 minutes.

4. Add jaggery, boiling it till it dissolves. Mix the rice flour with a little water and pour into the mixture. Boil the mixture till the whole is well blended, and remove from fire and cool.

Serves 5

CARROT PACHIDI

Carrot Salad

½ cup	whole green gram dal
3	carrots
5	green chillies
½	lime
	Salt to taste

1. The sprouts have to be prepared 2 days ahead. Soak the whole green gram dal for 24 hours. Tie up in a muslin cloth and allow to rest overnight. The dal will sprout by the next morning, if not, sprinkle water and keep for one more night.

2. Clean the carrots and grate coarsely. Wash the sprouts gently and add to the grated carrot. Add the green chillies finely chopped. Add the juice of the lime, salt and mix thoroughly.

Chill before serving.

Note: *The sprouts can be prepared from any whole dal, and refrigerated till required. They are very nutritious and tasty when combined with vegetables.*

Serves 6

NON-VEGETARIAN
CURRIES & FRIES

Curries and gravies are piquant sauces which team very well with soft cooked rice or with Indian breads. Tamilian curries have a delectable tang, and are moderately spiced to enhance the taste of meat or vegetables. The vegetarian curries are as tasty as the non-vegetarian ones, and a number of recipes in this book are from traditional non-Brahmin families. I have, however, included some of the all time favourites of both Brahmin and non-Brahmin communities, strictly vegetarian, and some of them dal based.

The *varavuls* which are dry curries or fries, are somewhere in between the dry roasted dishes and the gravies, and have sufficient masala to enable one to eat the dishes with rice or s or chappatis. The popular termin-ology for these *varavuls* is 'side dishes' which comple-ment the *entrees.*

When the term 'mutton' is used, it denotes the meat of a young goat, as in India the meat of sheep is not favoured, being tougher. Traditional Hindu families do not eat beef or pork, and these meats have been omitted even though the Christian communities partake of them. Every part of the goat is used for curries, right from the head and brain to the hooves.

Places near the sea coast offer a wide variety of fish and sea food is popular in Tamil Nadu. Fish is part of the daily diet, and chicken was considered a delicacy and cooked on special occasions. Today, with the accent on health, red meat is avoided and chicken cooked more frequently. For the confirmed non-vegetarian, vegetarian days are frequent in the Hindu calendar, so that vegetarian recipes are very much in demand!

Today the unfertilised egg is treated as vegetarian, and many vegetarians look upon eggs as concessions! Being versatile as well as rich in vitamins, a variety of dishes made with egg offer good substitutes for the meats.

MUTTON

MARGANDAM RASAM

Breast Bone Soup

200 gm	spare ribs
2 tbsp	oil
6	black pepper corns
1 large	onion (sliced)
2 cloves	garlic
1 tsp	grated ginger
1 large	tomato
¼ tsp	turmeric powder
	Salt to taste

1. Wash and clean the ribs.

2. Heat oil in a pressure cooker, and add pepper corns. When they crackle, add the onions and fry till transparent.

3. Add chopped garlic and grated ginger and fry for a minute. Add chopped tomato and fry for 2 minutes.

4. Pour 4 cups of water and add turmeric powder and salt to taste. Add the spare ribs and pressure cook for 20 minutes.

5. Strain and serve hot with toasted bread.

Serves 4

MURUNGAKKAI KARI KOZHAMBU

Mutton Curry with Drumsticks

500 gm	mutton
4	drumsticks
250 gm	potatoes (optional)
½	coconut
2 tsp	poppy seeds
2	medium sized onions (chopped)
2	medium sized tomatoes (chopped)

Seasoning

2 tbsp	oil
1 tbsp	ghee
1 heaped tsp	vadagam*
8	curry leaves
½ tsp	turmeric powder
3 heaped tsp	coriander powder
2 heaped tsp	chilli powder
2 heaped tsp	ginger-garlic paste
	Salt to taste
1 tsp	thick tamarind pulp

To Garnish

½ cup	chopped coriander leaves

1. Clean and wash mutton and chop into pieces.

2. Wash drumsticks, remove fibre and cut into 3" pieces.

3. Grate coconut, and grind to a fine paste with poppy seeds.

4. Heat oil and season with vadagam* and curry leaves. Add onions and fry till they are golden, add tomatoes and fry till the whole mixture is well blended. Add turmeric powder, coriander and chilli powder, ginger-garlic paste and 2 tablespoons of water so that all the ingredients are blended well. Stir fry.

5. Add the mutton and continue to fry, stirring well till the oil rises to the top. Add 2 cups of water and salt, and pressure cook for 15 minutes with potatoes.

6. Mix the coconut and poppy seed paste with 2 cups of water and add to the mutton curry. Add drumsticks and boil the curry till it is cooked. Add tamarind pulp and allow the curry to simmer for 5 minutes.

7. Garnish with coriander leaves. Serve hot with s.

* Instead of vadagam, 3 cloves, 2 (1" pieces) cinnamon, 2 cardamoms, may be used.

Serves 6-7

115

MADURAI MURUNGAKKAI KOZHAMBU

Madurai Mutton Curry with Drumsticks

750 gm	mutton
250 gm	spare ribs
3	drumsticks

Masala 1

4 heaped tbsp	coriander powder
1 tbsp	chilli powder
1 tsp	turmeric powder
½ tsp	pepper powder

Masala 2

1 tsp	cummin seeds
1 tsp	fennel seeds
½ tsp	mustard seeds
½ tsp	fenugreek seeds
A pinch of	asafoetida powder
1	lime sized ball tamarind
4 tbsp	oil
3 large	onions (chopped fine)
3	medium sized tomatoes
	Salt to taste

1. Wash the mutton and the spare ribs, and chop into small pieces.

2. Remove the fibre from the drumsticks, and chop into 3" pieces.

3. Grind fine with a little water the ingredients listed under Masala 1.

4. Broil the ingredients listed under Masala 2 and grind to a fine paste.

5. Place the asafoetida powder in a cup of hot water and add the tamarind. Mix well and extract the juice.

6. Heat the oil in a pressure cooker, and add onions. When browned, add tomatoes, Masala 1 and Masala 2 and stir constantly on low heat. Add meat, tamarind extract and salt, and water if necessary and pressure cook for 15 minutes.

7. Open the cooker after the pressure has subsided and add the drumsticks, seal cooker and switch off as soon as the pressure is reached, the indication being a loud hiss.

Note: *If a pressure cooker is not used for cooking the mutton, tamarind juice should be added after it is cooked, and drumsticks added last as it is a fragile vegetable.*

Serve with plain rice

Serves 7

BADAM CURRY KOZHAMBU

Almond Mutton Curry

*T*his curry is prepared in the same way as mutton drumstick curry, except that for seasoning, only whole spices are to be used.

Potatoes may be substituted for drumsticks.

Coconut should be substituted by ½ cup shelled, deskinned almonds which are ground to a paste with poppy seeds. To deskin almonds, soak them in hot water for 10 minutes.

This curry, which is thick, may be served with s or chappatis, or eaten with plain rice.

CHOPS KARI KOZHAMBU

Mutton Chops Curry

500 gms	mutton chops
1 tsp	turmeric powder
2 tbsp	curd
2 tbsp	oil
2 tbsp	ghee

To Grind

Masala 1

2 heaped tsp	coriander seeds
2 heaped tsp	black whole pepper
½ tsp	fennel seeds
1" piece	cinnamon
3	cloves
2	cardamoms
1	medium sized onion (sliced)
6	green chillies

½ cup	chopped coriander leaves
1" piece	ginger
15 flakes	garlic

Masala 2

½	coconut
2 tsp	poppy seeds
2	medium sized tomatoes

Seasoning

2	bay leaves
½"	piece cinnamon
1	clove
1	cardamom
2	medium sized onions (sliced)
	Salt to taste
½	lime

1. Clean the chops and flatten with mallet. Smear with turmeric powder and curd and set aside.

2. Heat 2 teaspoons of oil in a pan and sauté the ingredients listed under To Grind (Masala 1), for 2 minutes. Grind to a fine paste.

3. Grind Masala 2 to a fine paste.

4. Heat the remaining oil in a pressure cooker and sauté the whole spices listed under Seasoning. Add the sliced onions and fry till they are transparent.

5. Add the ground masala 1 and sauté for 3 minutes. Add the chops and stir well and continue frying till the masala is well blended and the oil rises to the top.

6. Add Masala 2, and pour water to make a gravy consistency. Add salt to taste.

7. Pour remaining ghee over the curry and pressure cook for 15 minutes.

Serve hot with plain rice or bread.

Serves 6 - 7

119

INJI KARI KOZHAMBU

Ginger Mutton Curry

500 gms	tender mutton
3 tsp	ginger paste
1 tsp	chilli powder
1 tsp	coriander powder
½ tsp	turmeric powder
	Salt to taste
1	coconut

Seasoning

2 tbsp	oil
1" piece	cinnamon
2	cloves
2	cardamoms
2	onions (chopped)
6	green chillies (slit lengthwise)
1 tsp	ginger-garlic paste

To Garnish

½ cup	chopped coriander leaves

1. Clean the meat and cut into small chunks.

2. Mix the ginger paste, chilli and coriander powder, turmeric and salt, and marinate the meat in the mixture, for 1 hour.

3. Grate the coconut and extract ½ cup of thick milk, and 2 cups of thin milk.

4. Heat the oil in a pressure cooker, and season with whole spices. Add the chopped onions and chillies, and fry till the onion is transparent.

5. Add the ginger garlic paste and fry on low heat for 2 minutes. Add the meat with the marinade and sauté for 10 minutes on low heat.

6. Pour the thin coconut milk over the meat and pressure cook for 15 minutes.

7. Add the first coconut milk and allow to boil for 5 minutes.

Garnish with chopped coriander leaves just before serving.

Serve hot with plain rice or puris or chapatties.

Serves 6

PACHAI MASALA KARI KURMA

Green Mutton Curry

500 gm	mutton
¾ cup	thick beaten curd
5 (250 gm)	potatoes
250 gm	mochakka (shelled beans), optional

To Grind

Masala 1

2 tsp	ghee
3	cloves
1" piece	cinnamon
¼ tsp	fennel
1 tbsp	coriander seeds
1 large	onion (chopped fine)
10	green chillies
1 cup	chopped coriander leaves

Masala 2

½	coconut
2 tsp	poppy seeds
2 large	tomatoes

Seasoning

2 tbsp	oil
1" piece	cinnamon
3	cloves
4	cardamoms
8	curry leaves
6	mint leaves
2 large	onions (sliced)
2	green chillies (slit)
1 tsp	turmeric powder
	Salt to taste
½	lime

1. Clean and wash the mutton and chop into bite size pieces. Marinate with the curd and set aside for half an hour.

2. Skin the potatoes, and quarter them and place in a vessel of cold water along with the mochakkas.

3. Heat the ghee in a heavy vessel and sauté cloves, cinnamon, fennel and coriander seeds. Add onions and green chillies and sauté till the onions turn transparent. Add ginger-garlic paste and sauté for a minute. Add coriander leaves, mix and remove from heat. Grind all these ingredients to a fine paste. (Masala 1)

4. Grind the coconut and poppy seeds with the tomatoes to a fine paste. (Masala 2)

5. Heat oil in a heavy vessel, and season with whole spices. Add curry leaves and mint. Lower the heat and add sliced onions, and slit green chillies, and sauté till onions turn a light brown. Add turmeric powder and salt, and fry for 2-3 minutes.

6. Add the mutton with the curd and masala 1, and fry on very low heat till the oil rises to the top. Care should be taken not to burn the masala, or it will lose its green colour.

7. Add potatoes and masala 2, and pressure cook for 10 minutes till the potatoes and the meat are done.

Serve hot with coconut rice.

Note: *If a pressure cooker is not used to cook the meat, Masala 2 can be added after the meat and potatoes are cooked, boiled for about 8 minutes on low heat, and taken off the fire.*

Serves 6

THENGAI PAAL KARI KOZHAMBU – 1

Coconut Milk Mutton Curry – 1

500 gm	mutton
¾ cup	thick curd
2 tbsp	oil

To Grind
Masala 1

3	cloves
1" piece	cinnamon
2 tsp	coriander seeds
1 tsp	fennel seeds
1 small	onion
10	green chillies
2" piece	ginger
½ pod	garlic
½ cup	coriander leaves
1	medium sized tomato

Masala 2

1	coconut
2 tsp	poppy seeds

Seasoning

3	bay leaves
3	cloves
1" piece	cinnamon
2	cardamoms
2	green chillies (slit lengthwise)
1 large	onion (chopped)
2	medium sized tomatoes
½ tsp	turmeric powder
	Salt to taste
250 gm	potatoes
	(skinned and cut into quarters)

124

To Garnish

½ cup   chopped coriander leaves

1. Clean and wash mutton, and chop into pieces. Marinate in beaten curds.

2. Heat 2 teaspoons of oil in a pan and sauté the ingredients listed under Masala 1, in the same order. Grind to a fine paste, and set aside.

3. Grate the coconut, and grind half a cup of it with the poppy seeds to a fine paste. (Masala 2)

4. Extract milk from the rest of the coconut and set aside.

5. Heat the rest of the oil and add ingredients listed under Seasoning. Sauté until the onions turn transparent, then add meat and fry for 5 minutes.

6. Add the ground masala 1, turmeric powder and salt and fry for 5 minutes longer. Add 2 cups of water and the coconut and poppy seed paste, blending it into the gravy.

7. Add potatoes, and allow the curry to boil till meat and potatoes are cooked.

8. Add coconut milk, and simmer for 8 minutes.

Garnish with chopped coriander leaves.

Serve hot with rice or chapattis.

Serves 6

CHETTINAD VARUVAL KOLA

Meat Balls Chettinad Style

500 gm	mince meat
1 tsp	oil
1 tblsp	oil

To Fry and Grind

100 gm	cashew nuts
100 gm	fried Bengal gram dal
2 tsp	poppy seeds
5	cloves
1½ tsp	fennel seeds
5	red chillies
6	shallots
1 pod	garlic
10	green chillies
1	coconut(grated)
1	egg
	Salt to taste
2 cups	oil

1. Clean and wash the mince meat and fry for 3-4 minutes in 1 teaspoon of oil. Grind to a paste.

2. Heat one tablespoon of oil in a kadai and fry all the ingredients listed.

3. Grind to a paste, mix with beaten egg and salt. Form into lime sized balls and deep fry in hot oil.

Serve hot.

Makes about 38 meat balls

Carrot Pachidi (Salad) shown here with Rasam (Lentil Soup),
Thayir Vadai (Lentil Patties in Curd) and sprouted lentils.

1. Carrot Pachidi (Carrot Salad)
2. Rasam (Lentil Soup)
3. Thayir Vadai (Lentil Patties in Curd)
4. Sprouted Lentils

Chuppal Curry (Broomstick Mutton Curry) is one of the unforgettably delicious surprises of Tamilian cooking.

1. Chuppal Curry (Broomstick Mutton Curry)
2. Ingredients on skewers for Chuppal Curry
3. Puris (Fried Indian Bread)

THENGAI PAAL KARI KOZHAMBU - 2

Coconut Milk Mutton Curry – 2

500 gm	mutton
½ cup	curd
2 large	coconuts

Seasoning

2 tbsp	oil
1 tbsp	ghee
3	cloves
3	cardamoms
2 (1" pieces)	cinnamon
2 large	onions (chopped fine)
2 tsp	chilli powder
2 tsp	coriander powder
1 tsp	turmeric powder
2 tsp	garlic paste
1 tsp	ginger paste
	Salt to taste

1. Clean and wash mutton and cut into pieces. Pour beaten curd over it and allow to marinate.

2. Grate coconuts and extract 1½ cups thick milk, and 2 cups thin milk.

3. Heat the ghee and oil in a pressure cooker, and add whole spices. Add onions, chilli, coriander and turmeric powder, and garlic and ginger paste, and fry for 5 minutes on low heat.

4. Add the mutton and fry till oil rises to the top.

5. Add the thin coconut milk, turmeric powder and salt and pressure cook for 15 minutes.

6. Add thick coconut milk, and boil the whole for 5 minutes till curry becomes thick and golden.

Serve hot with chapattis.

Serves 6

CHUPPAL KARI KOZHAMBU

Broomstick Mutton Curry

250 gm	mutton
3	medium sized onions
2 large pods	garlic
50 gm	ginger
8	green chilles

To Grind

1 tsp	oil
2 tbsp	coriander seeds
10	red chillies
1 tsp	cummin seeds
1 tsp	black pepper corns
¼ tsp	fenugreek seeds
2 (1" piece)	cinnamon
2	cloves

Seasoning

4 tbsp	oil
1" piece	cinnamon
2	cloves
2 large	onions (sliced finely)
4	green chillies (slit)
2 heaped tsp	ginger paste
2 heaped tsp	garlic paste
1 large	tomato
½ tsp	turmeric powder
	Salt to taste
1	marble sized ball tamarind

1. Wash mutton, and cut into cubes. Remove the skin from the onions, and quarter them. Remove the layers and set aside. Separate the garlic flakes, and remove the skin. Scrape the ginger, wash and slice into rounds ¼" thick. Remove the stems from the green chillies, and cut each chilli into 3 pieces.

2. Take about 6-8 broomsticks*, clean and scrape them. Sharpen one end to a point. 6" metal skewers may also be used. Thread the above vegetables and mutton on the broomsticks alternately.... 1 mutton cube, 1 flake garlic, 1 piece green chilli, 1 onion piece, 1 ginger slice, and repeat the process, tightly packing these, to cover 5" of the broomstick. Trim the ends, but not too close to the threaded ingredients. Set aside.

3. Heat the oil in a pan, and fry the rest of the ingredients listed under To Grind. Grind to a fine paste.

4. Heat the oil in a wide pan, and season with cinnamon and cloves. Add the onions and green chillies, and sauté till the onions turn a rich brown. Add the paste of ginger and garlic and fry for 2-3 minutes. Add the tomatoes and turmeric powder and fry till the tomatoes are cooked and are well blended with the rest of the masala. This might take about 5-7 minutes, on low heat.

5. Add a cup of water, allow it to boil and gently lower the threaded broomsticks into the gravy. When the mutton is nearly cooked, add salt to taste and the juice extracted from the tamarind.

6. Allow the gravy to simmer till fairly thick, and the mutton is cooked.

Serve with plain rice.

Serves 5

* Bromsticks are taken from coconut fronds. My husband's grandmother, who frequently made this curry, had silver skewers made to thread the ingredients!

KARI PERATEL

Mutton Gravy
laced with Fenugreek and Dill Leaves

A most delectable soup-like curry, peratel is one of the traditional dishes and a favourite with a section of the Mudaliars. Lightly spiced, it has the strong flavour of two kinds of 'greens' — dill and fenugreek — with distinctive aromas of their own. Vegetarian peratel is equally tasty using knolkol, potatoes, beans and peas. Other combinations which can be used as an alternative to the main ingredients listed below are:

1. minced meat instead of meat,
2. a combination of string beans, potatoes and peas if knolkol and mochakka are not available.

500 gms	mutton
250 gms	knolkol
250 gms	potatoes
250 gms	mochakka
2 cups	fresh dill
½ cups	fresh fenugreek leaves
1 tsp	turmeric powder
2 tsp	ginger-garlic paste
2 tsp	chilli powder
3 tsp	coriander powder
2	medium sized onions (chopped)
2	medium sized tomatoes (chopped)
	Salt to taste

Seasoning

2 tbsp	oil
1" piece	cinnamon
2	cloves

1. Clean and wash the meat, and cut into pieces. Pare the knolkol, cut into half and slice thinly. Wash the potatoes, remove the skins and quarter them. Shell the mochakka.

2. Remove the thick stems from the dill and wash the remaining part of the bunch thoroughly. Chop very finely to make up approximately 2 heaped cups. Remove the leaves from the stems of the fenugreek, wash and chop finely to make ½ cup.

3. Pressure cook the meat for 15 minutes along with the knolkol, potatoes and mochakka, adding turmeric powder, ginger-garlic paste, chilli and coriander powder, half the onions, all of the chopped tomatoes and salt to taste.

4. Heat the oil in a vessel, and season with cinnamon and cloves. Add remaining onions and fry till light brown. Add the chopped greens, and fry till liquid evaporates, and the greens become moderately dry. Add this to the meat gravy and simmer gently for 7 minutes till the greens are cooked.

Serve hot with chapattis.

Serves 5

THALAI KARI

Sheep Head Curry

1	sheep's head
½ tsp	turmeric powder
	Salt to taste

To Grind
Masala 1

6	red chillies
1 tbsp	coriander seeds
1 tsp	black pepper corns

Masala 2

½ cup	grated coconut
2	tomatoes (chopped)
1 large	onions (sliced)
2 tsp	ginger-garlic paste

Seasoning

2 tbsp	oil
3	cloves
2 (1" pieces)	cinnamon
1 large	onion (sliced)
½ cup	chopped coriander leaves

1. The sheep's head should be skinned and cleaned thoroughly at the butcher's, and chopped into large pieces. Pressure cook for ½ an hour with turmeric powder and salt, till soft.

2. Broil the red chillies, coriander seeds, and pepper corns and grind to paste. (Masala 1)

3. Grind the coconut, the tomatoes and onions to a fine paste, and add the ginger garlic paste and blend. (Masala 2)

4. Heat oil in a heavy pan and season with the spices. Fry the onions till they are brown. Add Masala 1 and fry for 3 minutes.

5. Add Masala 2, and fry for 2 minutes on low heat. Transfer this masala to the meat, mix well and allow the gravy to simmer for 10 minutes on low heat.

6. Squeeze the juice of the lime and garnish with chopped coriander leaves.

Serve hot with rice or dosais.

Serves 6

AATTU KAAL KOZHAMBU

Sheep Trotters Broth

When you purchase the trotters from the butcher's, get him to clean the pieces, singe the hair and chop the upper portion of the hooves so that cooking would be made easier. In the old days the trotters would be made to cook on low heat the whole night through!

4	trotters
½ cup	red gram dal
½ tsp	turmeric powder
	Salt to taste

Seasoning

2 tblsp	oil
1	bay leaf
3	cloves
2 (1" pieces)	cinnamon
2	medium sized onions (sliced)
1 large	tomato(chopped)
2 tsp	ginger-garlic paste
2 tsp	chilli powder
2 tsp	coriander powder
½ cup	chopped coriander leaves

1. Pressure cook the trotters and the dal with turmeric powder and salt in 4 cups of water for 30 minutes. Drain the soup, set aside and add 1 ½ cups of water and pressure cook for another 15 minutes. Both the liquids may be mixed together.

2. Heat the oil in a heavy large pan, and season with bay leaf and the other whole spices. Brown the sliced

onions, and add the tomatoes. Add the ginger-garlic paste and the chilli and coriander powder, and
sauté till oil rises to the surface. Add the trotters
and the broth and boil the whole till the masala is
absorbed.

3. Garnish with coriander leaves just before serving.

    Note: *Paya has to be served piping hot otherwise the*
    gelatine will make it very sticky. It is best served with appams.

Serves 6

KYMA URUNDAI KARI KOZHAMBU

Meat Ball Curry (Mudaliar)

For the Meat Balls

500 gm	mince meat
½ tsp	turmeric powder
½ cup	fried Bengal gram powder (powdered fine)
½ tsp	chilli powder ⎫
1 tsp	coriander powder ⎬
	OR
4	green chillies ⎫
½ cup	coriander leaves ⎬
2	cloves (pounded fine)
2 (1" pieces)	cinnamon (pounded fine)
1 tsp	ginger-garlic paste
1	egg (beaten) OR
	a slice of bread dipped in water and squeezed out
	Salt to taste

Seasoning

2 tbsp	oil
8	curry leaves
2	cloves
2 (1" pieces)	cinnamon
2	cardamoms
2 large	onions (chopped fine)
1 ½ tsp	chilli powder
2 tsp	coriander powder
3 tsp	ginger-garlic paste

To Grind

2 large	tomatoes
½	coconut
2 tsp	poppy seeds

2 tsp	cummin seeds
	Salt to taste
½	lime

To Garnish

| ¼ cup | chopped coriander leaves |

Preparation of Meat Balls

1. Wash the minced meat, and squeeze out the water. Grind to a paste. Add turmeric powder, ginger-garlic paste, chilli powder, coriander powder, cloves and cinnamon, powdered fried Bengal gram, beaten egg and salt to taste. Knead the mixture well and form small compressed lime sized balls, and set aside in a large plate and cover.

Preparation of Gravy

2. Heat the oil in a heavy vessel, and add curry leaves, and whole spices followed by chopped onions. Sauté till onions are transparent.

3. Add chilli and coriander powders, and the ginger-garlic paste, cooking on low heat till the oil rises to the surface.

4. Grind to a fine paste the ingredients listed under To Grind and add to the above, adding salt to taste for the gravy, and blending it well. Add enough water to make it a pouring consistency.

5. Let the gravy simmer for 10 minutes, and carefully add the mince meat balls, one by one.

6. Cover the vessel and cook for 20 minutes on low heat or until meat balls are cooked and the curry thickens.

Add the juice of the lime, remove from heat, and garnish with chopped coriander leaves.

Serve hot with coconut rice.

Serves 6

KOLA KOZHAMBU

Meat Ball Curry (Chettiar)

For the Mince Meat Balls

500 gm	mince meat
150 gm	cashew nuts
5 tblsp	fried Bengal gram dal
2 tsp	poppy seeds
1 ½ tsp	fennel seeds
5	cloves
6	green chillies
5	red chillies
3	onions
1 pod	garlic
1	coconut (grated)
1	egg
	Salt to taste

FOR THE GRAVY
To Grind

15	red chillies
100 gm	coriander seeds
½ tsp	turmeric
2 tsp	fennel seeds
1 tsp	cummin seeds
2 tsp	poppy seeds
4	cloves
3	onions
1 pod	garlic
2 tbsp	oil
4 large	tomatoes (chopped)
	Salt to taste
1	marble sized ball tamarind

Preparation of Mince Meat Balls

1. Clean the mince meat and wash. Squeeze out the water and grind to a paste.

2. Grind the other ingredients listed below it to a fine paste. Add beaten egg, add to the mince meat and mix well. Form into lime sized balls.

Preparation of Gravy

3. Grind all the 8 ingredients listed under To Grind, to a paste.

4. Heat oil in a heavy vessel and add the above ground masala, fry for 3 minutes. Add the tomatoes, and fry till blended. Add salt, and tamarind extract made up to 1 cup and boil the mixture for 5 minutes.

5. Add 2 cups of water and when it begins to boil, add prepared mince meat balls and let the gravy simmer for 15 minutes till the meat is cooked and the gravy becomes thick.

6. Garnish with coriander leaves.

Serve hot with plain rice or chapattis.

Serves 6

PODALANGAI KARI KOZHAMBU

Mince Meat Stuffed Snake Gourd Curry

1 long	(800-900 gm)snake gourd
4	cloves
4 (1" pieces)	cinnamon
2 tbsp	oil
1 large	onion (chopped fine)
8	green chillies
1½ tsp	ginger-garlic paste
¼ tsp	turmeric powder
500 gms	mince meat (washed and cleaned)
	Salt to taste
1 cup	chopped coriander leaves
2 slices	bread

To Grind

½	coconut
2 tblsp	poppy seeds
4	tomatoes (pureéd)

For the Gravy

6	curry leaves
1 large	onion (sliced)
2	green chillies (slit)
½ tsp	chilli powder
½ tsp	coriander powder
1 tsp	cummin seed powder
1 ½ tsp	ginger-garlic paste

1. Lightly scrape the surface of the snake gourd. Cut into 3" pieces, and scoop out the centres.

2. Grind to paste or powder 3 cloves and 3 pieces of cinnamon.

3. Heat 2 teaspoons of oil in a frying pan, and lightly fry chopped onion and green chillies. When the

142

onions become transparent, add the spice powder or paste, ginger-garlic paste, and turmeric powder and sauté for 2 minutes.

4. Add the washed mince meat and salt, and mix well. Add enough water to cook and keep on stove till the mince meat absorbs the water entirely. Add ½ cup chopped coriander leaves.

5. Stuff the mince meat tightly into each snake gourd piece, leaving ½" on both ends.

6. Dip bread in water, squeeze out water and crumble into pieces. Pack these into both ends of the gourd pieces.

7. Grind to a fine paste the coconut and poppy seeds.

8. Pureé the tomatoes.

9. Heat remaining oil in a heavy vessel and season with remaining whole spices and curry leaves. Add chopped onions and green chillies, till onions are light brown. Add chilli, coriander and turmeric pow-der, cummin seed powder, and ginger-garlic paste and fry for a couple of minutes.

10. Add enough salt for the gravy, add the coconut and poppy seed paste and tomato pureé. Simmer for about 5 minutes.

11. Add the snake gourd pieces and simmer till the vegetable is cooked, or pressure cook for 5 minutes.

Serve hot with coconut rice (page 32) or tomato rice (page 88).

Serves 6

MUTTAI GHOSE KYMA KOZHAMBU

Cabbage-Mince Meat Curry

½ -¾ kg	cabbage (whole)
½ tsp	salt
250 gm	mince meat
½ tsp	turmeric powder
1 heaped tsp	ginger-garlic paste
	Salt to taste
2 tbsp	oil
2	cloves
1" piece	cinnamon
3 (60 gm)	onion (chopped fine)
3	green chillies (chopped fine)
½ tsp	chilli powder
¾ tsp	coriander powder

For the Gravy

2 tbsp	oil
2	cloves
2 (1" pieces)	cinnamon
2	cardamoms
1	onion (sliced)
¾ tsp	coriander powder
1 ½ tsp	chilli powder
½ tsp	turmeric powder
1 heaped tsp	ginger-garlic paste
2	medium sized tomatoes (chopped)

To Grind

½	coconut
2 tsp	poppy seeds

1. Remove 10 leaves from the cabbage, making sure they are not damaged, but fresh and green. Any size of cabbage may be used, and once the leaves are removed, the rest can be stored for later use for

any other dish. Slice off part of the centre thick stem from the back, but take care to keep the leaves whole without any tear or gash. Wash thoroughly. Boil enough water in a wide vessel, to submerge the leaves. Add ½ teaspoon salt. Add the cabbage leaves to the boiling water and allow it to simmer for 3 minutes. Remove from water and set aside on a plate.

2. Pressure cook the washed mince meat along with the 3 ingredients listed below it.

3. Heat the oil in a kadai and season with the whole spices. Add the onions and chillies and let them brown lightly. Add chilli and coriander powder, and fry for 2 minutes. Add the boiled mince meat along with the liquid and dry fry the whole.

4. Place 1 tablespoon of mince meat in a cabbage leaf and roll inwards, tightly. Fasten with two cloves, or tie lightly with a string. Repeat the process till all the mince meat is used . Set aside on a plate.

5. Heat the oil in a heavy vessel, and season with whole spices. Add chopped onion and brown lightly. Add the coriander, chilli and tumeric powders. Add ginger-garlic paste and chopped tomatoes, and fry for 3 minutes on low heat.

6. Grind coconut and poppy seeds to a fine paste and add to the above. Add 2 cups of water and salt to taste, and simmer till the raw smell disappears and the curry is thickening. Gently slip the cabbage rolls one at a time into the curry and simmer for 5 minutes, or till the cabbage leaves are cooked.

7. Garnish with chopped coriander leaves and serve with chapattis.

Serves   6-7

SUNDIYA

Fried Meat Balls Wrapped in Plantain Bark

500 gm	mutton
1 tsp	oil

To be powdered individually

1 dsp	fennel seeds
1 dsp	poppy seeds
1" piece	cinnamon
½" piece	nutmeg
4	cloves
4	cardamoms
15	cashew nuts

(A)

2 tsp	oil
½	coconut (grated fine)
15	shallots (chopped fine)
1 pod	garlic (chopped fine)
	Salt to taste
4 dsp	fried gram dal (powdered)
3 tsp	chilli powder
½ tsp	turmeric powder

1. Clean and wash the meat and cut into pieces. Boil in salted water till tender and set aside. Drain the mutton broth, and shred the meat finely.

2. Fry each of the 7 ingredients listed (A) in a teaspoon of oil, and powder each individually.

3. Fry the grated coconut in oil till light brown and crisp. Fry the chopped onion and garlic till brown, and set these aside.

4. Add the prepared powders to the shredded meat, and add the grated coconut, onion and garlic. Add salt to taste, fried gram dal powder, chilli and turmeric powders. Add a little of the broth if necessary to make a stiff dough. Form into balls.

5. Fasten each ball with strips of plantain bark, criss crossing each other. Deep fry in hot oil.

Serve hot.

Makes about 38 balls

KYMA PUTTU

Dry Fried Mince Meat

500 gm	mince meat
250 gm	green peas (optional)
2 heaped tsp	ginger-garlic paste
½ tspn	turmeric powder
	Salt to taste

Seasoning

2 tbsp	oil
1 tbsp	ghee
2	cloves
2 (1" pieces)	cinnamon
4	medium (60 gm) onions (chopped fine)
10	green chillies (chopped fine)
1	lime
½ cup	chopped coriander leaves

1. Wash and clean mince meat. Shell peas and wash them.

2. Pressure cook the mince meat and peas with ginger-garlic paste, turmeric powder and salt to taste in half a cup of water for 10 minutes.

3. When the cooker is opened, set aside the peas and boil the meat till all the water is absorbed. Cool, and grind the meat fine.

4. Heat the oil and ghee in a kadai, and add cloves and cinnamon. Add the onions and green chillies and fry till onions are light brown. Add the ground meat and the peas and dry fry on low heat.

5. Add the juice of the lime and garnish with chopped coriander.

Serve hot with chapattis.

Serves 5

KYMA VADAI

Deep Fried Meat Balls

500 gm	mince meat
½ tsp	turmeric powder
	Salt to taste

To Grind

1 tsp	ginger paste
1 tsp	garlic paste
4	cloves
1" piece	cinnamon
1 heaped tsp	cummin seeds
½	grated coconut
4	medium sized onions
6	green chillies
½ cup	fried gram dal
2 small	eggs
½ cup	chopped coriander
2 cups	oil

1. Wash the mince meat and squeeze out excess water. Add turmeric powder and salt.

2. Grind together to a smooth paste the ginger-garlic paste, cloves, cinnamon and cummin seeds, and add to the meat mixture. Pressure cook the mixture for 10 minutes adding a cup of water. Open the cooker and cook the mixture till all the water is absorbed. Cool and grind the meat mixture to a slightly coarse paste.

3. Grind the coconut separately to a paste with minimum of water used for grinding.

4. Chop the onions and green chillies very fine. Powder the gram dal finely.

148

5. Add the coconut paste, onions, green chillies,gram dal powder, and egg to the meat, and knead the mixture.

6. Form small balls the size of a lime and flatten slightly. Arrange the prepared vadais on a plate.

7. Heat the oil to smoking point, and fry the vadais in batches till golden brown. Moderate the heat so that the vadais are cooked evenly. Drain, and place on kitchen paper to absorb excess oil.

Note: As kids our favourite combination was, apart from popping hot vadais, virtually off the kadai, rice mixed with keerai kozhambu with a dollop of ghee, and vadais eaten between mouthfuls!

149

Serves 7

KYMA VARUVAL

Mince Meat Fry

250 gm	mince meat
250 gm	green peas
1	medium sized onion (chopped)
1	medium sized tomato (chopped)
1 heaped tsp	ginger-garlic paste
1 tsp	chilli powder
1 ½ tsp	coriander powder
¼ tsp	turmeric powder
	Salt to taste
½ cup	water

Seasoning

2 tblsp	oil
2 medium sized	onions (sliced fine)
1" piece	cinnamon
2	cloves

To Garnish

½ cup	coriander leaves

1. Wash the mince meat and squeeze out excess water.

2. Shell peas and cook them in salted water.

3. Add chopped onion, tomato, ginger-garlic paste, chilli, coriander and turmeric powder, and salt to taste to the mince meat. Mix and pressure cook for 10 minutes with half a cup of water.

4. Heat oil in a kadai, and season with cinnamon and cloves. Add the sliced onions and fry till light brown. Add the cooked mince meat and peas along with the water and keep on heat till medium dry, stirring occasionally.

The mince meat can be fried dry or retained as a thick sauce to be eaten with chapattis.

Garnish with chopped coriander.

Serves 4

Note: *Interesting variations – substitute peas for string beans, ladies fingers, cabbage or potatoes.*

VENDHIKEERAI KYMA VARUVAL

Mince Meat with Fenugreek Leaves

Follow the same recipe as Kyma Varuval. When seasoning, after the onions are browned, add ½ cup cleaned and washed fenugreek leaves and fry on low heat for 5-7 minutes till the greens get discoloured, then proceed in the same way.

Do not garnish with coriander leaves.

Serves 4

CHOPS KARI VARUVAL

Fried Mutton Chops

Use recipe for Chops Kari Kozhambu, omitting the coconut and poppy seeds paste. Simmer on low heat till most of the gravy is absorbed and a thick masala is left with the meat. Serve with Vendhikeerai Rice (recipe page 79) or with bread or chapatties.

Serves 5

MUTTON CHOPS
(IN EGG BATTER)

1 kg	mutton chops
To Grind	
2 tsp	oil
10	red chillies
1 tsp	fennel seeds
1 tbsp	cummin seeds
¼ tsp	poppy seeds

152

1 tsp	whole black peppercorns
1" piece	ginger
2 pods	garlic
4 tbsp	grated coconut
4 tbsp	oil
1"	cinnamon
3	cloves
3	cardamoms
4 large (80 gm)	onions (chopped)
3 large	tomatoes (chopped)
½ tsp	turmeric powder
	Salt to taste

For the Batter

2	eggs
¼ cup	chopped coriander leaves
3 tsp	refined flour

1. Flatten the chops slightly with a wooden mallet, clean, wash and set aside.

2. Heat 2 teaspoons of oil in a frying pan and lightly saute the ingredients listed under To Grind, up to garlic (inclusive). Grind to a paste with grated coconut.

3. Heat 4 tablespoons of oil in a heavy vessel, and season with the listed whole spices. Add the onions, and when golden brown, add the tomatoes and the ground masala. Add turmeric powder and salt. Sauté the masala till the oil separates. Add chops, and 2 cups of water, and cook till done. Keep on heat till dry.

4. Make a batter with the eggs, coriander leaves and refined flour. Dip the chops one by one into this batter, coating it well and deep fry in hot oil.

Serve with bread and soup

Serves 4

MOOLAI VARUVAL

Brain Fry

3	brains (of goat or sheep)
½ tsp	turmeric powder
½ tsp	salt
½ cup	fenugreek leaves

Seasoning

1 ½ tbsp	oil
1 tsp	ghee
2	cloves
2 (1" pieces)	cinnamon
3	onions (chopped fine)
1 large	tomato (chopped)
1 tsp	chilli powder
1 ½ tsp	coriander powder
1 heaped tsp	ginger-garlic paste
	Salt to taste

1. Wash brains thoroughly. Heat a cup of water, add ¼ teaspoon turmeric powder and salt. When it starts to boil, add the cleaned brains. Cook for about 5-7 minutes on medium heat till the brain feels firm. Peel off the outer thin membrane of the brains, drain the water and chop into small pieces.

2. Wash fenugreek leaves, chop and cook in 2 tablespoons of water for about 5 minutes. Drain the water and set the fenugreek leaves aside.

3. Heat the oil and ghee in a karai and season with cloves and cinnamon, and add chopped onion, frying till it turns light brown.

4. Add the fenugreek leaves and fry for 3 minutes.

5. Add chopped tomatoes, chilli and coriander powder, rest of the turmeric powder, ginger-garlic paste, and fry on low heat for 5 minutes till all the ingredients are integrated.

6. Add the brain, mix well with the gravy, and simmer on low heat till the gravy becomes very thick.

Note: *If fenugreek leaves are not available, garnish with chopped coriander leaves before removing the brain from the stove.*

Serve hot with chapattis.

Serves 5

KYMA SAMOSA

Mutton Puffs

½ recipe	kyma puttu (peas are optional)
2 cups	wheat flour
1 cup	refined flour
	Salt to taste
2 cups	sunflower oil

1. Mix wheat flour, refined flour, and salt. Make a well in the centre of the flour. Heat one tablespoon of oil and pour it in the well. Knead well with water to make a stiff but pliable dough.

2. Roll out into thin rounds, and using a cutter or an inverted steel plate with straight rims with a diameter of 4-5". Cut into rounds.

3. Place a tablespoon of puttu in one half of the round, and apply water at the edge of this half circle. Cover this half with the other, pressing the edges so that they seal. Trim the edges with a cutter wheel. Prepare the samosas this way till the dough and the puttu are used up.

4. Heat the oil in a kadai to smoking point, and gently lower the samosas one at a time till there are about three in a batch. Flip over so that the other side also browns lightly.

5. Drain the cooked samosas of oil using a ladle with holes, and place on kitchen paper to absorb excess oil.

Serve hot with mint chutney.

Serves 8   Makes about 36 samosas

EERAL VARUVAL

Liver Fry

1	goat's liver
2 tsp	vinegar
1 tsp	black pepper corns (powder)
½ tsp	ginger-garlic paste
¼ tsp	turmeric powder
	Salt to taste
1 small	onion (chopped)
1 tbsp	oil

1. Wash the liver, cut into small pieces. Marinate with vinegar, freshly ground pepper, ginger-garlic paste, turmeric powder and salt to taste, for 2 hours.

2. Fry onions in the oil till light brown. Add the liver and the marinade and fry on medium heat till water evaporates.

Note: *Liver cooks in an amazingly short time. If kept too long a time on heat, it overcooks and becomes hard.*

Serve with bread, or as a cocktail snack.

Serves 4

CHICKEN

Till recently, chicken was considered a delicacy to be eaten on special occasions. With the rising cost of mutton, and health consciousness chicken dishes are made more frequently than before. Most of the recipes for mutton can be adapted effortlessly for chicken, except that chicken tastes better cooked without vegetable accompaniments. If at all, peas or potatoes may be added to the fries.

For instance, the recipe for Mutton Drumstick Curry which is a basic mutton curry, can be adapted, except that you do not add drumsticks, but substitute it with potatoes, if you wish. Likewise Mutton Almond Curry and Mutton Chops Curry take chicken beautifully. For a 500 gram mutton recipe, increase the quantity of ginger-garlic paste by ½ teaspoon. The Green Masala Mutton Curry recipe is delicious when chicken is substituted for mutton.

In the good old days, when the young women of the family gave birth to a children, it meant a great deal of organising for the elders — the women in the household. Apart from the intense massage with herbal oils and the hot rejuvenating baths followed by incense in the room and garlic skin on hot coal, menus were painstakingly planned as food formed an important part in recouping.

Pathiyam saapad (restrictive food) was given to the lactating mother as long as she nursed the baby and all spicy food was taboo. Pepper was the only concession. After the protracted bath with hot water in which neem leaves and turmeric soaked, the young woman was given chicken soup with a teaspoon of brandy as a pick-me-up after the rigours of the bath!

While the best pieces of chicken were reserved for the 'pepper fry', some of the bony pieces of chicken, gizzard and wings were made into soup. It is believed even today that the nursing mother produces more milk if she is given a diet of green dill in some form or the other, and shark, seasoned with plenty of garlic.

KOZHI RASAM

Chicken Soup

250 gm	chicken pieces
¼ tsp	turmeric
3 flakes	garlic
	Salt to taste
1 tbsp	oil
4	black pepper corns
1 large	onion (sliced)
2	tomatoes (chopped)

1. Wash the chicken pieces and pressure cook for 20 minutes with turmeric powder, chopped garlic and salt to taste, adding 3 cups of water.

2. Remove the flesh and discard the bone. Chop or shred the chicken into small pieces and set aside.

3. Heat the oil in a vessel, and add the onion, sauting it till it turns a golden brown. Add the tomatoes, sauting till they are cooked and blended with the onion.

4. Add the chicken broth, topping it with more water to make 5 cups of soup. Boil for 10 minutes. Strain the soup, and sprinkle shredded chicken over each serving.

Serve piping hot.

Serves 5

Note: *The traditional way of making chicken broth is to place the chicken pieces in cold water in a vessel with small bits of onion & garlic, bring it to boil & simmer on low heat for 2 hours, then proceed as in 2,3,4.*

KOZHI VARTHA KOZHAMBU

Chettinad Chicken Curry

1 large (1 kg)	chicken
1 large	coconut

Seasoning

3 tbsp	oil
2 (1" pieces)	cinnamon
2 tsp	fennel seeds
1 cup	curry leaves
3 large(60 gm)	onions (sliced finely)
3 tsp	ginger-garlic paste
3 tsp	chilli powder
3 tsp	coriander powder
½ tsp	turmeric powder
3 large	tomatoes
	Salt to taste
1	marble sized ball tamarind

1. Clean chicken, cut into 12 -14 pieces and wash thoroughly.

2. Extract 1½ cups of thick milk from grated coconut and 1½ cups of thin milk.

3. Heat oil in a heavy vessel and season with cinnamon and fennel seeds. Add the curry leaves, sauté and add onions.When they turn golden brown, add ginger-garlic paste, chilli, coriander powder, and turmeric. Sauté for 2 minutes, add chopped tomatoes, and stir fry till tomatoes are well blended.

4. Add chicken pieces and salt and sauté till oil rises to the top.

5. Pour the thin milk over the chicken, and cook covered on low heat.

6. When the chicken is tender, add the thick coconut milk, and the thick juice extracted from the tamarind.

7. Simmer for 5 minutes, and remove from heat.

Serve hot with steamed rice, tomato rice or chapatties.

Serves 7-8

KOZHI UPPU VARUVAL

Chettinad Chicken Fry

1 large(1 kg)	chicken
	Salt to taste
½ tsp	turmeric powder
2 tbsp	oil
1 tsp	fennel seeds
10	red chillies (broken into pieces)
4 large	onions (chopped)
2 large	tomatoes (chopped)

1. Clean the chicken, wash, and cut into 12 pieces. Smear salt and turmeric powder and set aside.

2. Heat the oil in a heavy vessel, and season with fennel and broken red chillies. Fry the onions till golden brown. Add the chopped tomatoes, and fry till ingredients are well blended.

3. Add the chicken pieces and sauté. Keep sprinkling hot salt water, while frying. Cook till chicken is tender and a golden brown, adding a little extra oil if the chicken has not browned.

This dish is an excellent accompaniment for a pulao or a curry.

Serves 8

*Chicken is often served as a delicacy. Kozhi Velai Kozhambu (White Chicken Curry)
is featured here with tomato rice, a curd based salad and shelled mocjakka beans.*

1. Chicken Velai Curry
2. Tomato Rice
3. Shelled Mocjakka in brass scoop
4. Thayir Pachidi

Sea fish is favoured by Tamilians, specially the fleshy fish varieties with a central bone. Meen Varuval (Fish Curry) is seen here, along with puris and a spinach curry.

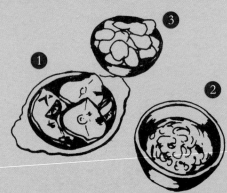

1. Meen Varuval (Fish Curry)
2. Keerai Kozhambhu (Spinach Curry)
3. Puris (Fried Indian Bread)

KOZHI MOLAVU VARUVAL

Chicken Pepper Fry

1 large(1 kg)	chicken
1	lime
3 tsp	ginger-garlic
½ tsp	turmeric powder & Salt to taste

To Powder

2 dsp	whole black pepper
2 dsp	cummin seeds
3	cloves
2 (1" pieces)	cinnamon

Seasoning

3 tbsp	oil
10	curry leaves
2 large	onions (thinly sliced)

To Garnish

½ cup	coriander leaves

1. Remove the skin from the chicken, joint into 12 pieces. Remove bony pieces, gizzard and wings to make about 250 gm and reserve for soup.

2. Extract the juice from the lime, mix with ginger-garlic paste, turmeric powder and enough salt for the chicken, and rub the paste on the pieces and set aside. Broil the ingredients listed under To Powder and powder them coarsely.

4. Heat the oil in a kadai, and season with curry leaves. Add the onion and when golden brown, add the powdered spices. Sauté for 2 minutes, and add the chicken. Fry on low heat for about 5 minutes. Add half a cup of water and allow the chicken to cook.

5. When the chicken is tender enough, keep on heat till all the water is absorbed. Continue sauting till chicken browns evenly.

6. Garnish with coriander leaves.

Serve as a side dish with a vegetable curry.

Serves 5

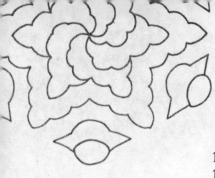

KOZHI VELAI KOZHAMBU

White Chicken Curry

1 large(1kg)	chicken
1 large	coconut
2 tsp	oil

To Grind

1 large	onion
1½" piece	ginger
20 flakes	garlic
1" piece	cinnamon
2	cloves
2	cardamom
½ tsp	fennel seeds
8	green chillies
1 tsp	coriander seeds
1 tsp	cummin seeds
25 gm	cashew nuts
1 cup	thick curd

Seasoning

2 tblsp	oil
1	bay leaf
2	cloves
1" piece	cinnamon
2 small	onions (sliced)
	Salt to taste
1	lime

To Garnish

½ cup	chopped coriander leaves

1. Clean the chicken, remove skin and extra fat. Cut into 14 pieces, and wash thoroughly.

2. Grate the coconut, extract 1½ cups thick milk, and 1½ cups thin milk.

3. Heat 2 teaspoons oil in a pan and lightly sauté all the ingredients listed under To Grind. Take care not to brown the onions, and remove from heat as soon as they turn transparent. Cool, and grind to a fine paste.

4. Beat the curd lightly and blend in the masala. Coat the chicken with this masala and set aside.

5. Heat oil in a heavy vessel and season with bay leaf and the whole spices, followed with sliced onions. When the onion turns transparent, add the chicken with the masala and fry lightly.

6. Add the thin coconut milk and salt,and reduce the heat. Cover with a lid and simmer till the chicken is cooked. Add thick coconut milk and simmer for 10 minutes.

7. Remove from heat, add juice extracted from the lime, and mix well.

8. Garnish with coriander leaves.

Serve hot with steamed rice or chapattis.

Serves 8

FISH

$\mathcal{S}$ea fish is favoured by the people in Tamil Nadu, especially those living in the coastal areas. What is preferred is fish with more of flesh, and just a central bone, like sear fish and pomfret.

The smaller ones like salmon, mackerel, and sardines are tastier when they are roasted with spicy, mouth-watering masala. The curries are hot, and made with tamarind. The Tamils make their fish curry traditionally in a mud vessel which is seasoned with rice water first. The pot is reserved only for the making of fish curry, and the curry is tastier on the second day, probably due to the flavour of the mud vessel!

Dried fish, which is relished, is available in plenty, and is enjoyed in the form of curries or fries by those who don't mind the strong odour.

Tamilians enjoy delicacies made from prawn and crab, and shark is particularly popular as it is believed to be beneficial for lactating mothers.

MEEN KOZHAMBU

Fish curry

250 gm	fish (sear or pomfret)

To Grind

1 cup	grated coconut
2	medium sized onions
6	black peppercorns
8	red chillies
1 tbsp	coriander seeds
10 flakes	garlic
10	curry leaves
1 large	tomato
1	lime sized ball tamarind

Seasoning

2 tbsp	gingelly oil
2 tsp	vadagam*
1	onion (finely chopped)
8 flakes	garlic
1 tsp	turmeric powder
	Salt to taste

1. Clean the fish and cut into medium sized pieces.

2. Dry roast half the quantity of coconut in a kadai.

3. Remove the skin from 1 onion, insert a knife into it and roast in the fire till it turns brown but not charred.

4. Grind to a fine paste the entire quantity of coconut, the roasted onion, 1 raw onion, red chillies, coriander seeds, 10 cloves garlic, curry leaves and tomato.

5. Extract thick juice from the tamarind, and set aside.

6. Heat the oil gently in a heavy vessel, add vadagam*, 1 chopped onion and garlic. Fry till light brown, and add the ground masala and fry till the masala is blended and the oil rises to the surface. Add tamarind extract, turmeric powder, salt and 4 cups of water. Simmer on low heat till the curry becomes thick. Add the fish pieces and simmer for 5 minutes, and remove from fire.

Serve with idlis, or plain rice.

Serves 5

Vadagam may be substituted with 1 tsp mustard seeds, 1 tsp split black gram split dal, ½ tsp cummin seeds, 1/4 tsp fenugreek seeds and 8 curry leaves.

173

CHETTINAD MEEN KOZHAMBU

Chettinad Fish Curry

500 gm	seer fish

To Grind

15	red chillies
3 tbsp	coriander seeds (roasted)
1 tsp	fennel seeds
1 tbsp	poppy seeds

Seasoning

2 tbsp	oil
2 tsp	vadagam *
1 cup	shallots
2	tomatoes (chopped)
1 cup	curry leaves
1	lime sized ball tamarind
	Salt to taste
½ tsp	turmeric powder

1. Cut the fish into slices or chunks, clean and wash well.

2. Grind to a paste the ingredients listed under To Grind.

3. Heat oil in a heavy vessel, and season with vadagam*. If vadagam is not available, substitute with ½ teaspoon mustard, ½ teaspoon black gram dal, ½ teaspoon fenugreek seeds, ½ teaspoon fennel seeds.

4. Add shallots, tomatoes and curry leaves. Fry for a few minutes, and add the ground masala. Fry on low heat for 15 minutes, then add extract of tamarind, salt and turmeric powder, adding water to form a thin gravy.

5. Allow the gravy to boil for about 7-8 minutes. Slip in the fish pieces and let the curry boil for about 10 minutes, at the same time the fish should be cooked and the curry thick.

Serve with plain rice.

Serves 7

SORRA KOZHAMBU

Shark Fish Curry

500 gm	shark fish
	(silver white variety, *paal sorra*)
1 tsp	turmeric powder

Sauté and grind fine

2 tbsp	sesame oil
4 tsp	black pepper corns
1 large	onion (chopped)
15 flakes	garlic
2 medium size	tomatoes
½ tsp	turmeric powder
100 gms	tamarind
3 tsp	vadagam
8	curry leaves
	Salt to taste

1. Clean and cut the shark into large pieces. Heat water in a vessel and when it starts boiling add tumeric powder and the shark, and boil till the fish is cooked, this would take between 3 to 5 minutes. Drain the water immediately, and remove the skin from the fish. Wash gently again, as you will find grit on the underside of the skin. Cut into medium sized pieces.

2. Heat 2 teaspoons of oil in a kadai, and add pepper corns, and when they crackle, add chopped onion and sauté. Add garlic and sauté for a minute. Add chopped tomatoes and turmeric powder, and stir fry for 2 minutes. Grind the fried ingredients to a fine paste.

3. Extract thick juice from the tamarind, and set aside.

4. Heat the remaining oil in a vessel, and season with vadagam* and curry leaves. Add the ground masala and salt and stir fry till oil rises to the surface.

5. Add the tamarind juice and 2 cups of water and simmer on medium heat till the gravy thickens. Add the fish pieces and simmer for 5 minutes.

Serve hot with steamed rice or idlis.

Serves 5

KARVAD KOZHAMBU

Salted Fish Curry

This curry is made with salted fish. Considered a great delicacy by Tamilians, it is shunned by some of the modern generation on account of its strong smell. Different kinds of fish are salted and preserved by sun drying. Salted fish is usually sold in 5" pieces, and can be preserved in airtight containers.

4 pieces	salted fish
250 gm	dehydrated mochakottai (optional)
1	lime sized ball tamarind
1 tsp	chilli powder
1 tsp	coriander powder
¼ tsp	turmeric powder
	salt to taste
2	medium sized onions
5	curry leaves
1 ½ tbsp	sesame oil
1 tsp	vadagam
1	medium sized onion (sliced)
2	tomatoes

1. Wash the salted fish, and chop into 2" pieces.

2. Soak the mochakottai overnight and pressure cook for 15 minutes the next morning.

3. Extract juice from tamarind. Add chilli and coriander powder, turmeric powder and salt to taste to the juice.

4. Grind 1 onion and curry leaves coarsely and add it to the mixture.

5. Heat oil in a kadai, add vadagam and the remaining chopped onion till brown, and add tomatoes, frying till they are well blended.

6. Add the tamarind mixture and cooked mochakottai and boil for 10 minutes.

7. Add the salted fish, and simmer for 15 minutes till gravy becomes thick.

Serve hot with steamed rice.

Serves 5

NANDU KARI KOZHAMBU

Crab curry

6 medium sized	crabs
4 tbsp	oil

To Grind

1 large	onion
6 cloves	garlic
1" piece	ginger
1 large	tomato
7	green chillies
¾ cup	grated coconut
1 tsp	aniseed
1 tsp	poppy seeds
10	blanched almonds

To Powder

6	black pepper corns
3	cloves
1" piece	cinnamon
3	cardamom
½ tsp	cummin seeds
1 tsp	chilli powder
1 tsp	coriander powder
½ tsp	turmeric powder

Seasoning

1" piece	cinnamon
3	cardamom
10	curry leaves
	salt to taste

To Garnish

| ½ cup | chopped coriander leaves |
| 6 | lemon wedges |

1. Break open the large crab shells and discard the fibrous tissue which might be adhering to the shell. Pound the claws if they are large, breaking them into convenient sizes to eat. Leave the claws as they are if they are smaller.

2. Chop the onion, garlic, ginger, tomato and green chillies into small pieces.

3. Heat a tablespoon of oil, and fry the above ingredients till the onions are translucent.

4. Dry roast the grated coconut, aniseed, poppy seeds, and almonds, and grind them with the fried ingredients to a fine paste.

5. Heat the remaining oil in a heavy bottomed vessel, and season with cinnamon, cardamom and curry leaves. Add the ground paste, the spice powders (8 ingredients) and stir fry for 2-3 minutes. Add the crab meat and claws and mix well, stirring over heat till oil rises to the surface. Add 1 cup of water and salt to taste, and simmer until the crab is cooked.

6. Serve hot and garnish with chopped coriander leaves and lemon wedges. Serve with steamed rice.

Serves 6

YERRA VARUVAL

Fried Prawns

500 gms	prawns
250 gms	peas (optional)
2 tbsp	oil
4	medium sized onions(chopped fine)
2 tsp	chilli powder
3 tsp	coriander powder
½tsp	turmeric powder
1 ½ tsp	ginger-garlic paste
3	medium sized tomatoes
	Salt to taste
½ bunch	coriander leaves (chopped fine)

1. Shell prawns, devein, wash thoroughly and set aside. Cook the peas in salted water, till soft.

2. Heat oil in a kadai, and add onions. When they brown, add turmeric, chilli and coriander powder, ginger-garlic paste and fry for a couple of minutes. Add chopped tomatoes and sauté till the mixture is well blended.

3. Add salt, boiled peas and prawns and stir fry till the prawns are cooked. This should take about 10 minutes, take care not to overcook. The masala should also become thick and not flowing as in a curry.

4. Remove from heat, and garnish with chopped coriander leaves.

Serve hot with steamed rice or with chapatties.

Serves 5

MEEN VARUVAL – 1

Fried Fish – 1

1 kg	seer fish (or pomfret)
4	black pepper corns
6	curry leaves
½	onion
6 flakes	garlic
3 tsp	coriander powder
2 tsp	chilli powder
½ tsp	turmeric powder
	Salt to taste
1 tbsp	thick extract of tamarind
	Oil for frying

1. Clean the fish and cut into ¼" slices.

2. Lightly fry the peppercorns, curry leaves, onion and garlic in a teaspoon of oil, and grind to a paste.

3. Mix with the coriander, chilli and turmeric powder, salt and the tamarind extract.

4. Smear the fish slices with the masala, and allow to marinate for 2 hours.

5. Heat a flat griddle or tawa and pour a tablespoon of oil. Fry the fish slices on both sides till golden brown.

An excellent accompaniment to a main dish like a lentil curry.

Serves 4

MEEN VARUVAL – 2

Fried Fish – 2

500 gms	sardines or mackerel

To Grind

7 flakes	garlic
4	curry leaves
4	whole black pepper corns
1 tsp	cummin seeds

To Sauté

2 tbsp	oil
1 tsp	mustard seeds
1 tsp	split black gram dal
5	curry leaves
1 small	onion
½ tsp	turmeric powder
3 tsp	coriander powder
2 tsp	chilli powder
1 tbsp	tamarind extract
	Salt to taste
2	limes or lemons cut into wedges
½ bunch	coriander leaves

1. Clean the fish thoroughly, scraping off scales if any, removing the intestine, and cutting off the edge of the tail. The full form of the fish is retained as far as possible.

2. Grind to a coarse paste the ingredients listed under To Grind.

3. Heat oil in a heavy griddle or tawa, and add mustard seeds and black gram dal, followed by curry leaves. When it crackles, add the chopped onions, turmeric, coriander and chilli powders. Add the masala paste and salt, blend with 4-5 tablespoons of water. Add the tamarind extract, and salt.

4. Allow the mixture to simmer for 3-4 minutes. Add the whole fish, and gently turn so that the masala covers the entire fish. Cover with lid so that the masala and moisture are absorbed. Open the lid and sauté till the fish is dry and crisp.

Serve with lemon wedges and chopped coriander leaves.

Serves 5

SORRA PUTTU

Shark Fish Crumble

500 gms	shark fish
½ tsp	turmeric powder
200 gms	peas (optional)
4	onions
8	green chillies
2 tbsp	oil
20 flakes	garlic
2 tsp	ginger-garlic paste
½ tsp	turmeric powder
½	lime

To garnish

1 bunch	coriander leaves (finely chopped)

1. Chop the fish into large pieces and wash and clean thoroughly. Heat water in a vessel, add when it comes to a boil, add turmeric powder and the fish pieces. Boil till fish is cooked taking care not to overcook. It should take 3-5 minutes. Drain off the water and remove the skin. Wash gently to remove any grit sticking to the surface. Cool, and crumble the flesh into a mixture that resembles breadcrumbs. The backbone of the fish may be retained, and cut into 1 ½" pieces, and added to the crumble or puttu.

2. Shell the peas and cook in salted water till soft. Set aside.

3. Chop onions and green chillies.

4. Heat the oil in a heavy vessel, and add the chopped onions and chillies. When the onions become transparent, add turmeric powder and sauté till the

raw smell disappears. Add garlic flakes, and sauté till they become light brown. Add ginger-garlic paste and sauté for 1 minute.

5. Add the puttu and salt to taste and stir vigorously so that the ingredients are evenly distributed. Add peas and sauté on low fire till all the water is absorbed.

6. When the puttu is still slightly moist and soft, take off the heat, add the juice of the lime, and mix well. Garnish with chopped coriander leaves.

Sorra puttu is delicious eaten with hot steamed rice and a dollop of ghee, or plain as a side dish.

Serves 5-6

EGGS

ven the strictest of vegetarians, at least some of them, concede to eating eggs. Eggs are so versatile that they can be adapted to any of the non-vegetarian kurmas or fries.

OMELETTE KOZHAMBU

Omelette Curry

4	eggs
	Salt to taste
2 tsp	oil
1 small	onions (finely chopped)
1	green chillies (finely chopped)
1 tbsp	chopped coriander

To Grind
Masala 1

1 small	onion
5	green chillies
1 tbsp	coriander seeds

4	black peppercorns
12 flakes	garlic
1" piece	ginger
½ cup	chopped coriander leaves
5 leaves	mint

Masala 2

½	coconut
1 tsp	poppy seeds
2	medium sized tomatoes

Seasoning

2 tbsp	oil
3	cloves
2 (1" pieces)	cinnamon
2	cardamoms
6	curry leaves
1 large	onion (sliced fine)
½ tsp	turmeric powder
½ cup	curd
	Salt to taste

To Garnish

¼ cup	chopped coriander leaves

1. Break eggs into a bowl, add salt and whisk till creamy.

2. Heat the oil in a frying pan, and lightly fry chopped onion and chopped green chillies. Add to egg mixture. Add chopped coriander leaves.

3. Heat oil in a tawa or griddle and spoon the mixture onto it, folding both edges when done, making 12 individual omlettes. Cut into 2" pieces and set aside.

4. Grind to a smooth paste the ingredients listed under To Grind, Masala1.

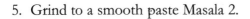

5. Grind to a smooth paste Masala 2.

6. Heat remaining oil in a heavy vessel and season with whole spices and curry leaves. Add chopped onion, and when brown add the green masala paste (Masala 1) and sauté on low heat till the oil rises to the top.

7. Add turmeric powder, beaten curd and salt and enough water to form a thin gravy.

8. Add the coconut-poppy-tomato paste (Masala 2) and simmer till the gravy becomes thick. Add omelette pieces and simmer for a further 5 minutes.

9. Garnish with chopped coriander leaves.

Serve hot with chapattis or puris.

Serves 6

MUTTAI VARUVAL

Egg Fry

6	eggs
2 tbsp	oil
5	curry leaves
2	cloves
½" piece	cinnamon
2 large	onions (sliced lengthwise)
1 ½ tsp	chilli powder
2 tsp	coriander powder
½ tsp	cummin powder
½ tsp	pepper powder
½ tsp	turmeric powder
2 large	chopped tomatoes
1 tsp	ginger-garlic paste
	Salt to taste

To Garnish

½ cup	chopped coriander leaves

1. Boil the eggs and slice into halves lengthwise.

2. Heat oil in a kadai, season with curry leaves and whole spices. Add sliced onions and sauté till brown.

3. Add the 5 spice powders listed and sauté well. Add tomatoes, ginger-garlic paste and salt and stir fry till the whole masala is well blended. Add the eggs and mix well while still on the stove.

4. Remove from heat and garnish with chopped coriander.

Delicious with chapattis or puris.

Serves 6

Eggs make versatile components in of many dishes. Seen here is Muttai Kozhambu (Egg Curry), along with sauted greens and mutton chops.

1. Muttai Kozhambu (Egg Curry)
2. Keerai Poriyal (Sauted Greens)
3. Chops Kari Varuval (Fried Mutton Chops)

Grams, beans and lentils form an intrinsic part of the daily menu.

1. Soyikeerai
2. Vendhikeerai
3. Mochakka
4. Peratel

MUTTAI BAJJI

Egg Croquettes

6	eggs
1 cup	Bengal gram flour
¼ cup	rice flour
½ tsp	chilli powder
1 tsp	coriander powder
¼ tsp	turmeric powder
	Salt to taste
½ tsp	baking powder
	or soda bicarbonate
2 cups	oil for frying

1. Boil the eggs and quarter each egg.

2. Prepare a thick batter by combining the gram flour, rice flour, chilli, coriander and turmeric powder, salt and baking powder.

3. Coat each egg piece with the batter and deep fry in oil till golden brown.

4. Place on kitchen paper to drain off excess oil, and serve hot as a pre-dinner snack.

Serves 5

MUTTAI KOZHAMBU

Egg Curry

6	eggs
2 tsp	oil

To Grind
Masala 1

1 large	onion (chopped)
2	tomatoes (chopped)
1" piece	cinnamon
3	cloves
¼ tsp	fennel seeds
10	curry leaves
½ tsp	ginger-garlic paste

Masala 2

½	grated coconut

Seasoning

2 tbsp	oil
1 heaped tsp	vadagam*
	(or ½ tsp mustard seeds,
	½ tsp black gram dal,
	½ tsp cummin seeds
	¼ tsp fenugreek seeds
1 large	onion (chopped)
8	curry leaves
6 flakes	garlic
1	lime sized ball tamarind
1 heaped tbsp	chilli powder
1 heaped tbsp	coriander powder
½ tsp	turmeric powder
	Salt to taste

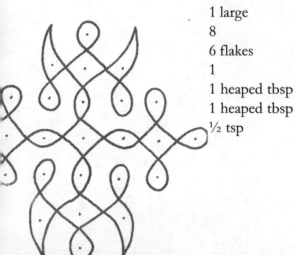

1. Hard boil the eggs, shell and make slits lengthwise, and set aside.

2. Heat the oil in a pan, and lightly sauté chopped onion, tomatoes, whole spices, fennel seeds and curry leaves, and grind to a fine paste with the ginger-garlic paste.

3. Grind the grated coconut to a fine paste.

4. Heat the oil in a heavy vessel, season with vadagam. Add chopped onion, curry leaves and garlic till the onions turn brown. Add thick extract of tamarind, chilli, coriander and turmeric powders, and mix well. Sauté for 2-3 minutes.

5. Add the coconut paste and allow to simmer till the oil rises to the surface. Add the eggs one at a time, and allow to simmer for about 7 minutes.

Serve hot with plain rice.

Serves 6

* Vadagam may be substituted by 3 cloves, 2 (1" pieces) cinnamon, 2 cardamoms.

MUTTAI PORIYAL

Egg Crumble

6	eggs
	Salt to taste
¼ tsp	turmeric powder
3 tbsp	oil
2 large	onions (finely chopped)
8	green chillies (finely chopped)
¼ cup	coriander leaves (finely chopped)

1. Break the eggs into a bowl, and whisk with salt and turmeric powder.

2. Heat oil in a kadai, and add onions, and green chillies. When the onions are turning light brown, lower the heat and pour the egg mixture into the kadai. Stir vigorously to break up the egg mixture, so that it resembles bread crumbs when cooked.

3. While still moist add the chopped coriander leaves, stir well and remove from heat.

Serve hot with chapattis.

Serves 4

CAULIFLOWER MUTTAI PORIYAL

Cauliflower Egg Crumble

All ingredients as in Muttai Poriyal, adding 1 cup cauliflower cut into small pieces and steamed.

Before the egg mixture is poured into the kadai, add the cauliflower. When the egg is added, mix well on low heat.

Garnish with chopped coriander leaves.

Serves 6

199

MURUNGAKEERAI MUTTAI PORIYAL

Egg Crumble with Drumstick Leaves

All ingredients as for cauliflower poriyal, only, substitute 1 cup tender drumstick leaves for cauliflower. Use only the leaves and discard the stems. Do not garnish with coriander leaves.

Serves 6

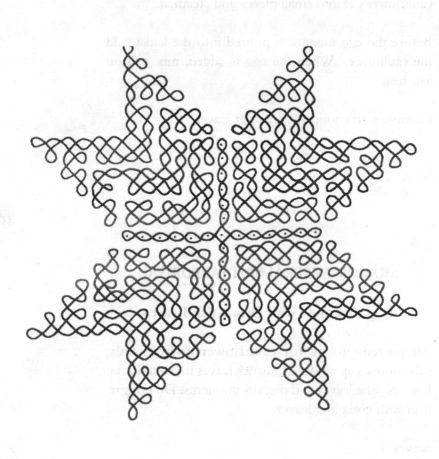

VEGETARIAN
CURRIES & FRIES

$\mathcal{M}$ore and more people throughout the world are beginning to realise that vegetarianism is a healthy concept. For those who have been fed on a totally non-vegetarian repast the change over is not too difficult when the recipes are followed faithfully, with vegetables substituted for meat, fish or chicken.

Indeed, the non-Brahmin vegetarian cuisine from Tamil Nadu is totally different from the delicious sambhars, kootus and poriyals that are part and parcel of Brahmin diets. Most of the curries with green masala, red masala and pepper masala double as vegetarian curries, potatoes being added instead of meat, accompanied by any other vegetable of your choice, like knolkol, carrots, beans, cabbage or peas.

If in a non-vegetarian household there is one confirmed vegetarian, as in ours, the curry is made with the basic

masala, a portion removed for the vegetarian and the vegetables added and boiled in the curry. The same procedure is followed for the other portion where meat, chicken or fish is added to the curry and cooked. I have found that this cuts out the tedium of making separate dishes for the vegetarians!

Spinach is a rich source of iron and the cheapest, and so many varieties are available for which the Western equivalent is not known. However, any kind of spinach can be used for the recipes given here, though the Tamil names for the greens are given here.

Some of the Tamilian vegetarian curries are tamarind based, and are made into well blended thick rich dark sauces, which can be preserved for days on end, and longer if refrigerated. It is usually eaten with rice, but makes delicious accompaniments for dosais, and idlis. Molavu kozhambu made with freshly ground pepper, is believed to be a good antidote for colds and sore throat, and a good digestive.

KAI KURMA

Vegetable Curry

Follow the recipe for Pachai Masala Kari Kozhambu (page 122). Substitute meat with vegetables: 100 gm carrots 100 gm string beans, 50 gm cabbage, 3 medium sized potatoes.

Dice the vegetables and proceed in the same way. Any other seasonal vegetables may be used.

Serves 6

PODALANGAI KOZHAMBU

Stuffed Snake Gourd Curry

Follow the recipe for Podalangai Kari Kozhambu (page 142). Substitute the mince meat for potato following the Potato Puttu recipe (page 237) and stuff into snake gourd. Make the curry as in the mince meat curry, folllowing the rest of the recipe.

Serve with plain white rice.

Serves 6

PODALANGAI CUTLETS

Snake Gourd Cutlets

Prepare the podalangai pieces in the same way as in the Podalangai Kari (Page 142), and stuff with potato crumble puttu (page 237). Prepare a thick batter with ½ cup of gram flour, 1 teaspoon chilli powder and salt to taste.
Dip the pieces into the batter, coat uniformly, and deep fry in 2 cups of oil till crisp. Spread on kitchen paper, and serve hot with tomato sauce.

Serves 8

KATHRIKKAI KADALAI PARUPPU KOZHAMBU

Brinjal Lentil Curry

¾ cup	Bengal gram dal
2 tbsp	oil
12	curry leaves
3	cloves
1" piece	cardamom
2	medium onions (sliced)
500 gm	young brinjals (each cut into 4 pieces)
1 heaped tsp	ginger-garlic paste
½ tsp	turmeric powder
1 ½ tsp	chilli powder
2 ½ tsp	coriander powder
	Salt to taste
1	marble sized ball tamarind

To Grind

½	coconut
2 tsp	poppy seeds
2	medium sized tomatoes
1/4 cup	coriander leaves

1. Clean the dal and pressure cook for 15 minutes. It should be cooked and soft but the form should be retained. Pour into a separate vessel.

2. Heat the oil in the same cooker after rinsing, and season with curry leaves and whole spices. Sauté the onion slices till they are light brown. Add brinjals. Sauté till they become discoloured and soft.

Add the ginger-garlic paste and the three powders listed. Sauté for 3 minutes, and add the cooked gram dal, and 2 cups of water to make a gravy consistency. Add salt to taste.

3. Add the extract of tamarind and allow the curry to simmer till oil rises to the surface, and till the brinjals are cooked.

4. Add the paste of coconut, poppy seeds and tomato, coriander leaves and ghee and simmer for 5 minutes.

Serve with dosais or chapattis.

Serves 6

KALLA VEETU KATHRIKKAI

Brinjal Curry (Chettiyar)

250 gm	brinjals
3	potatoes
1 large	tomato
2	medium sized onions
1	small pod garlic

To Grind

15	red chillies
3 tbsp	roasted coriander seeds
2 tbsp	grated coconut
1 tsp	poppy seeds

Seasoning

4 tbsp	oil
1 ½" piece	cinnamon
1 tsp	fennel seeds
8	curry leaves

To Garnish

A few sprigs	coriander leaves

1. Cut the brinjals, potatoes and tomato into cubes.

2. Chop the onions fine. Skin the garlic flakes and chop fine.

3. Grind to a fine paste the chillies and coriander seeds. Grind to a fine paste the coconut and the poppy seeds.

4. Heat the oil and season with ingredients listed. Add the onions and garlic. When the onions brown slightly, add the chilli-coriander paste and sauté for a few minutes. Add the brinjals and potatoes and fry for 5-7 minutes till the brinjal softens.

5. Add the coconut and poppy seeds paste and tomatoes. Add 3 cups of water, and boil till the vegetables are cooked. When the gravy becomes thick, remove from heat and garnish with coriander leaves.

Serve hot with ven pongal, dosais or idlis.

Serves 7 – 8

KATHRIKKAI KOSAMALLI

Thick Brinjal Sauce

250 gm	brinjals
2	medium sized potatoes
1	lime sized ball tamarind

Seasoning

3 tbsp	oil
1 tsp	mustard seeds
1 tsp	split black gram dal
8	curry leaves
1	pea sized piece asafoetida
100 gm	shallots (chopped fine)
6	green chillies (chopped fine)
1	medium sized tomato (chopped)

To Garnish

| ¼ cup | coriander leaves |

1. Roast the brinjals over fire or in the oven till soft. Remove skin and mash till smooth.

2. Boil potatoes, remove skin and mash till smooth.

3. Soak tamarind in 1 cup of water and extract the pulp.

4. Heat the oil in a heavy vessel and season with mustard seeds, black gram dal, curry leaves and asafoetida. Add the shallots and green chillies and allow to brown. Add tomatoes, and fry till soft.

5. Mix the mashed brinjals and the potatoes with the tamarind pulp, and add to the seasoned mixture. Blend the whole well, stirring continuously. Add water to form a gravy. Add salt and simmer on low heat till it becomes thick.

Garnish with coriander leaves and serve with dosais, idlis or venpongal.

Serves 6

KOZHAMBU

Lentil Balls in Curry Sauce

For the s

500 gm	Bengal gram dal
1 large	onion (finely chopped)
8	green chillies (finely chopped)
½ tsp	ginger-garlic paste
1 tbsp	curd
	Salt to taste
1 tsp	ghee

For the Gravy

2 tbsp	oil
3	cloves
2	cardamoms
1" piece	cinnamon
8	curry leaves
2	onions (sliced)
½ tsp	turmeric powder
¾ tsp	chilli powder
1 tsp	coriander powder
3	tomatoes (chopped)

To Grind

½	coconut
2 tsp	poppy seeds
2 cups	oil
½	lime

To Garnish

2 tsp	ghee
3 tbsp	cashew nuts
½ cup	chopped coriander

1. Soak the dal for 2 hours. Drain the water completely and grind to a coarse paste without using water. Add the rest of the ingredients listed under s, adding enough salt for the mixture. Form into tightly compressed lime sized balls, and arrange on a large plate.

2. Heat 2 tablespoons of oil in a heavy vessel, and season with the whole spices, curry leaves and sliced onion and fry till transparent. Add turmeric, chilli and coriander powders, and sauté for a minute. Add tomatoes and sauté till they are soft.

3. Grind to a fine paste the coconut and poppy seeds. Add to the above and add enough water to make a pouring consistency gravy and let the gravy simmer on low heat.

4. Meanwhile, heat the oil to smoking point in a kadai, and fry the prepared s. Add them gently to the simmering gravy and cook for 5 minutes before switching off the heat.

5. Squeeze the juice of the lime mixing it into the curry. Fry the cashew nuts a light brown in ghee.

6. Garnish with the coriander leaves and cashew nuts.

Serve with coconut rice.

Serves 6

MULANGI KADALAI KOZHAMBU

Radish – Chick Peas Curry

½ cup	chick peas
	Salt to taste
250 gm	white radish
2 tsp	oil

Seasoning

2 tbsp	oil
1 tsp	vadagam*
1	large onion (chopped)
½ tsp	turmeric powder
1 tsp	chilli powder
¾ tsp	coriander powder
1 ½ tsp	ginger-garlic paste
1 large	tomato (chopped fine)
½	lime sized ball tamarind

To Grind

| ½ | coconut |
| 2 tsp | poppy seeds |

To Garnish

| ¼ cup | coriander leaves |

1. Soak the chick peas overnight. Drain the water, pressure cook for 20 minutes till soft, but the shape is retained.

2. Scrape the radish, and slice into rounds. Heat the oil, and fry till light brown at the edges. Add to the chick peas.

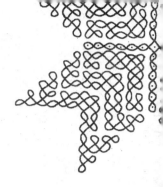

3. Heat oil in a heavy vessel and season with vadagam. Add onions and let them brown lightly. Add the turmeric, chilli and coriander powders and sauté. Add the ginger-garlic paste, and tomatoes, and sauté till the whole is well blended. Add the tamarind extract and boil till the oil rises to the surface.

4. Grind the coconut and the poppy seeds to a fine paste and add to the curry. Add the chick peas and radish, and more salt if needed, adding water if necessary to make a gravy consistency. Let the curry boil till the radish is cooked and the gravy thickens.

5. Garnish with chopped coriander leaves.

Serve hot with chappatis.

Serves 6

*Vadagam may be substituted by ingredients listed in previous recipes.

PARUPPU KARI KOZHAMBU

Lentil Cake Curry

1 cup	green gram dal
	Salt to taste
2 large	onions (finely chopped)
6	green chillies (finely chopped)
½ cup	coriander leaves (finely chopped)

1. Soak the dal for half an hour. Add salt and grind coarsely. Add the onions, green chillies and coriander leaves and mix it with the ground dal. Place the mixture in a colander, and flatten with the palm of your hand, to one inch thickness. Steam covered over boiling water for 7 minutes. Cut into squares.

2. Prepare the gravy in the same way as for Kozhambu and add the paruppu kari into the curry after it has been simmered. Cook for 7 minutes.

Serve with chapattis

Serves 6

Note: *The Paruppu Kari may be fried lightly in 2 tablespoons of oil and eaten plain instead of adding it to a curry.*

MANDI

Ladies Fingers Curry

500 gm	ladies fingers
2 tsp	oil

Seasoning

2 tbsp	oil
1 tsp	mustard seeds
1 tsp	split black gram dal
20	shallots
6	green chillies (slit)
1 pod	garlic (skinned)
½ cup	curry leaves
3 cups	water in which rice has been washed
3	tomatoes (chopped)
	Salt to taste
1	lime sized ball tamarind
1 cup	thick coconut milk, extracted from ½ coconut

1. Wash the ladies fingers, and wipe with a dry cloth. Chop into ½" pieces, and fry in 2 teaspoons of oil till it turns light brown. Set aside.

2. Heat oil in a heavy bottomed vessel, and season with mustard seeds and black gram dal. Add shallots, green chillies, and garlic, and sauté till shallots turn light brown. Add curry leaves and sauté till crisp. Add the washed rice water, tomatoes and salt to taste and boil for 5 minutes.

3. Add the fried ladies fingers, and tamarind extract, and boil till gravy thickens and the vegetables are cooked. Add the coconut milk, boil for 2 minutes and remove from heat. Serve hot with rice.

Serves 7

MURUNGAKKAI RAVAI KOZHAMBU

Drumstick Semolina Curry

| 4 | drumsticks |
| 1 | coconut |

Seasoning

2 tbsp	oil
2	cloves
2 (1" pieces)	cinnamon
1 large	onion (sliced)
6	green chillies (slit)
10 gm	cashew nuts
2 tbsp	fine semolina
1 tsp	ginger-garlic paste
	Salt to taste
½ cup	chopped coriander leaves

1. Remove the fibre from the drumsticks, chop off the ends, and cut into 3 inch pieces.

2. Grate coconut and extract 2 cups of thick milk, and 1 cup of thin milk.

3. Cook the drumsticks in the thin milk adding a little salt.

4. Heat the oil in a heavy vessel, and season with whole spices. Add the onion and green chillies and cashew nuts and fry till light brown. Add the semolina and ginger garlic paste, and fry for a minute. Add the cooked drumsticks with the the thin milk and salt. Add the thick milk and boil for 7 minutes. Add the coriander leaves and remove from heat.

Serve with bread or plain rice.

Serves 6 – 7

BEANS PAAL KOZHAMBU

Milk Curry with Beans

250 gm	string beans
2 tbsp	oil
2	cloves
2 (1" pieces)	cinnamon
1 large	onion (chopped)
6	green chillies (slit)
2 tbsp	fine semolina
1 tsp	ginger-garlic paste
	Salt to taste
2 cups	milk
½ cup	chopped coriander leaves

1. String the beans and cut into 1" pieces. Cook in 1 cup of water and salt.

2. Heat the oil in a vessel, and season with whole spices. Add the sliced onions and green chillies and fry till light brown. Add the semolina and fry for a minute. Add the ginger-garlic paste, and the cooked beans. Add the milk, and simmer on low heat till the curry thickens. Add more salt if required. Add the chopped coriander leaves, and remove from heat.

Serve with bread.

Serves 4

YENNAI KATHRIKKAI KOZHAMBU

Sautéd Brinjal Curry

500 gm	young purple brinjals

To Grind

1	medium sized onion
2 heaped tsp	cummin seeds
¼ tsp	fenugreek seeds
2 tbsp	chilli powder
3 tbsp	coriander powder
1 tsp	turmeric powder
½	coconut
1 heaped tbsp	poppy seeds
2 heaped tbsp	sesame seeds

Seasoning

¾ cup	oil
1 tsp	mustard
1 tsp	pepper
20	curry leaves
1 medium	onion (sliced)
2 large	tomatoes (chopped)
1 tsp	ginger-garlic paste
1	lime sized ball tamarind
	Salt to taste
4 tsp	powdered jaggery

To Garnish

¼ cup	chopped coriander leaves

1. Cut brinjals in 4 up to one inch of the stem leaving the stem intact.

2. Grind the first 6 ingredients listed to a fine paste and the next 3 ingredients separately.

3. Heat oil in a kadai to smoking point and season with mustard, pepper and curry leaves. Add the sliced onion, and the brinjals and fry till onions are brown and the brinjals discoloured. Add the first ground masala, tomatoes and ginger-garlic paste, and fry till the raw smell disappears and the whole is well blended, which would take about 5 minutes.

4. Pour a cup of water, add the second ground masala, the tamarind extract, salt to taste, jaggery and the required amount of water to make a thick gravy. Allow the curry to simmer till the brinjals become soft and cooked.

5. Garnish with coriander leaves.

Serve with Mutton Pulao (page 72).

Serves 6

VATHAL KOZHAMBU

Tamarind Gravy

1	lime sized ball tamarind (soak in water)

To Grind

1 tsp	fennel seeds
2 tsp	poppy seeds
2 tsp	coriander seeds
5	red chillies

Seasoning

2 tbsp	sesame oil
½ tsp	mustard seeds
½ tsp	split black gram dal
½ tsp	fenugreek seeds
15	shallots
2 pods	garlic
1 cup	curry leaves
3 (150 gm)	tomatoes (chopped)
½ tsp	turmeric powder
	Salt to taste

1. Extract the juice of the soaked tamarind and set aside.
2. Grind to a fine paste the ingredients listed, and blend into the tamarind extract.
3. Heat the oil in a heavy pan, and season with mustard seeds and black gram dal, and fenugreek seeds. When they crackle, add shallots and garlic and brown slightly. Add curry leaves, tomatoes and turmeric powder and fry till the whole is blended and the oil rises to the top.
4. Pour the tamarind mixture over the seasoning, add salt to taste and allow the curry to simmer till thick.

Serves 8

Note: *The following tamarind based curries (recipes pages 220-225) are accompaniments as rich tangy sauces and are not 'main' curries.*

SEERAGA KOZHAMBU

Tamarind-Cummin Gravy

1	lime sized ball tamarind (soaked in water)
2 tsp	cummin seeds

Seasoning

1 ½ tbsp	sesame oil
1 tsp	mustard seeds
1 tsp	split black gram dal
12	curry leaves
6 flakes	garlic
1 large	onion (chopped)
1	medium sized tomato (chopped)
2 tsp	chilli powder
1 tsp	coriander powder
½ tsp	turmeric powder
1 tsp	powdered jaggery

1. Extract juice from soaked tamarind.

2. Dry roast cummin seeds, powder and set aside.

3. Heat oil in a kadai, and season with mustard seeds and when they burst, add black gram dal, curry leaves, garlic and onion. When the onion browns, add tomato and sauté for 2 minutes. Add the chilli, coriander and turmeric powders.

4. Add the tamarind extract and 2 cups of water, and simmer the curry on low heat till it thickens.

5. Add the jaggery, and simmer for 5 minutes.

6. Add the cummin seed powder, mix and remove from heat.

Serves 6

MILAGU KOZHAMBU

Pepper Curry

1 lime sized ball	tamarind
	(soak in water for 1 hour)
1 ½ tsp	chilli powder
1 ½ tsp	coriander powder
½ tsp	turmeric powder
2 tsp	oil

To Grind

1 tbsp	whole black pepper corns
1 tbsp	coriander seeds
1 tbsp	red gram dal
1 medium sized	onion (chopped)
1 large	tomato (chopped)

Seasoning

2 tblsp	oil
1 tsp	vadagam*
12	curry leaves
1 medium	onion (chopped)
1 tsp	jaggery
	salt to taste

1. Extract the juice from the tamarind, and blend with the chilli, coriander and turmeric powder.

2. Heat the oil in a frying pan, and fry the ingredients in the order listed under To Grind. Grind to a paste, and add to the tamarind mixture.

3. Heat the oil in the kadai and season with vadagam and curry leaves. Add chopped onion and fry till golden brown. Add the tamarind mixture and allow to boil till it thickens.

4. Add jaggery and salt to taste and simmer the curry for 5 minutes and remove from heat.

Serve with plain rice.

Serves 6

* Vadagam may be substituted with the ingredients listed in previous recipes.

Note: *Specially recommended when one has a cold or a fever linked to a cold.*

223

VENDHIYAM KOZHAMBU

Fenugreek Gravy

1	lime sized ball tamarind (soaked in water)
2 tsp	chilli powder
1 tsp	coriander powder
½ tsp	turmeric powder
	Salt to taste

To Powder

1 tsp	fenugreek seeds
1 tsp	sesame seeds
1 tsp	poppy seeds

To Grind

2	medium sized onions
10	curry leaves

Seasoning

2 dsp	oil
1 heaped tsp	vadagam*
1	medium sized onion (chopped)
4	medium sized tomatoes (chopped)
1 heaped tsp	powdered jaggery

1. Extract juice from the tamarind, and add chilli and coriander powder, turmeric and salt.

2. Powder the ingredients listed and set aside.

3. Coarsely grind the onion and curry leaves.

4. Heat the oil in a heavy vessel and add vadagam, followed by onions. When the onion is transparent, add the tomatoes, sauting till they are cooked. Add the ground masala, and sauté for 2 minutes.

5. Add the tamarind mixture, and allow to simmer for 15-20 minutes till the curry starts thickening.

6. Add the jaggery and the powdered masala and allow to boil for 5-7 minutes.

Serves 6

* Vadagam may be substituted with the ingredients listed in previous recipes.

MORU KOZHAMBU

Curd Curry

2 ½ cups	curd
½ tsp	turmeric powder
	Salt to taste

To Grind

½ cup	grated coconut
6	green chillies
1" piece	ginger
2 tbsp	fried gram dal
1 tsp	cummin seeds

Seasoning

2 tbsp	oil
1 tsp	mustard seeds
1 tsp	split black gram dal
A pinch of	asafoetida
10	curry leaves
4	red chillies

To Garnish

| 2 sprigs | coriander leaves |

1. Beat the curd till smooth and mix with turmeric powder and salt to taste.

2. Grind to a smooth paste the ingredients listed under To Grind. Blend with the curd.

3. Heat the oil in a kadai, and season with mustard seeds, asaefotida, black gram dal, curry leaves and red chillies each broken in two. When the seasoning crackles, add the curd mixture. When the curry starts foaming, and when the first bubbles appear, switch off heat, and garnish with coriander leaves.

Serve with plain white rice.

Serves 6

Note: *Vegetables - cooked separately may be added like yellow pumpkin, ladies fingers (fried first).*

PARUPPU

Basic Red Dal

1 cup	red gram dal
3 flakes	garlic
¼ tsp	asafoetida
½ tsp	oil
½ tsp	turmeric powder

Seasoning

1 tbsp	oil
1 dsp	ghee
1 tsp	mustard seeds
1 tsp	split black gram dal
1 tsp	cummin seeds
12	curry leaves
1 large	onion (chopped)
4	green chillies (slit lengthwise)
2	medium sized tomatoes
	Salt to taste

To Garnish

½ cup	chopped coriander leaves

1. Pressure cook the dal with the 4 ingredients listed below it, for 5-7 minutes, with 4 cups of water. Mash coarsely.

2. Heat oil in a small pan and season with mustard seeds, black gram dal, cummin seeds and curry leaves. Add onion, and when transparent, add green chillies and tomatoes, and fry the ingredients till tomatoes become soft.

3. Add this to the cooked dal, boil for 3-4 minutes, and add salt to taste.

4. Garnish with chopped coriander.

Serve hot with chapattis or rice with ghee.

Serves 6

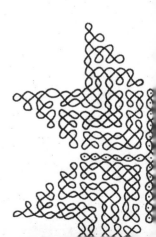

PACHAI PARUPPU

Green Gram Dal

Proceed exactly as for the previous recipe, substituting green gram dal for red gram dal. Care should be taken not to overcook the dal as it tends to become slimy when boiled for too long.

VENGAYYA SAMBHAR

Shallot Lentil Curry

½	lime sized ball tamarind (soaked for 1 hour or more)
1 cup	red gram dal
3 flakes	garlic
¼ tsp	powdered asafoetida
½ tsp	oil
½ tsp	turmeric powder

Seasoning

2 tbsp	oil
1 tsp	vadagam
6	curry leaves
250 gm	shallots (skinned)*
2 tsp	chilli powder
1 large	tomato (chopped)
	Salt to taste
1 tsp	ghee
2 tbsp	sambhar powder
¼ cup	chopped coriander leaves

1. Extract the juice from the soaked tamarind.

2. Pressure cook the dal in 4 cups of water along with the other ingredients listed below it for 5 minutes. Mash the dal coarsely.

3. Heat the oil in a small pan and season with vadagam and curry leaves. Add the whole shallots and brown lightly. Add the chilli powder and tomato and sauté for 2 minutes.

4. Add the tamarind extract and salt and let the gravy simmer till the shallots are cooked. Add the cooked dal and boil the gravy till well blended.

5. Add the ghee, sambhar powder and coriander leaves and remove from heat.

Serve hot with plain steamed rice or idlis.

Serves 6

*Sambhar onions (shallots) may be substituted by other vegetables like pumpkin, ladies fingers, radish or drumsticks. Vegetables that need longer cooking, can be pressure cooked after the seasoning is done.

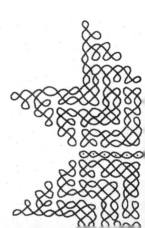

KEERAI KOZHAMBU

Spinach Curry

1 bunch (3 cups)	mollai keerai (greens)
1 heaped cup	red gram dal
½ tsp	turmeric powder
3 flakes	garlic
¼ tsp	asafoetida
½ tsp	oil
3 cups	water
1 large	onion (chopped)
4	green chillies (chopped)
1 large	tomato
	Salt
1	lime sized ball tamarind

Seasoning

2 tbsp	ghee
1 heaped tsp	vadagam*

1. Remove the leaves and tender stems from the bunch of greens, wash thoroughly and chop finely, and set aside.

2. Wash the dal, add turmeric powder, garlic, asafoetida, oil and water, and pressure cook for 15 minutes.

3. Open the cooker, add chopped greens, half of the chopped onions, green chillies, chopped tomatoes, salt and tamarind extract. Pressure cook for another 5 minutes.

4. Open the cooker when pressure is totally released, and drain the liquid into a vessel. Mash the greens well and pour back the liquid, so that the whole mixture is well blended.

5. Heat ghee in a frying pan and add vadagam, and the rest of the chopped onion. When the vadagam crackles, and when the onion turns light brown, add the seasoning into the spinach mixture. Boil for 5 minutes. Serve hot with plain rice and serve kyma vadais (recipe page 148) as a side dish.

Serves 6

* Vadagam may be substituted by ¼ teaspoon mustard seeds, ¼ teaspoon cummins seeds, ¼ teaspoon split black gram dal, $\frac{1}{8}$ teaspoon fenugreek seeds

231

KEERAI PORIYAL

Sautéd Greens

For this dish, greens which are called Arrakeerai *and* Sirukeerai *in Tamil, are used. They might not be available in some parts of India, but any kind of spinach used will be nearly as tasty!*

2	large bunches greens

Seasoning

1 tbsp	oil
½ tsp	mustard seeds
½ tsp	split black gram dal
6 flakes	garlic
2	red chillies (broken)
1 small	onion (chopped)
	Salt to taste

To Garnish

3 tbsp	grated coconut

1. Remove the leaves and tender stems from the bunch, wash, drain the water and chop finely.

2. Heat oil in a kadai, and season with mustard seeds, black gram dal, garlic and red chillies. When it crackles, add chopped onion and sauté till it turns transparent.

3. Add the greens, and the salt, sauté, and cover with a lid. Cook on low heat till water is absorbed and the greens are cooked.

4. Garnish with grated coconut.

Note: *As an alternative the dish can be garnished with ¼ cup cooked red dal, which should be lightly mixed into the cooked spinach. The dal is pressure cooked with a dash of turmeric powder, but all the water has to be absorbed. The dal should be soft, but the form retained and not mashed or over-cooked.*

Serves 4

PULI KEERAI

Greens in Tamarind Sauce

This is best done with Arakeerai which has a slightly bitter taste. The method is the same as for the previous recipe, only green chillies are substituted for red chillies, and one small tomato may be added.

When the greens are added, the extract of a lime sized tamarind ball is poured over it. When the greens are cooked the mixture is liquidised to form a thick dark green sauce which is delicious with hot rice and a dollop of ghee to cut out the bitter taste.

234

KADALAI PARUPPUSOYI KEERAI VARUVAL

Fried Lentil with Fresh Dill

2 cups	Bengal gram dal
¼ tsp	turmeric powder
	Salt to taste

Seasoning

3 tbsp	oil
2	cloves
1 (1" piece)	cinnamon
1 large	onion (sliced)
2 cups	fresh dill leaves (washed and chopped fine)
1 tsp	chilli powder
1 tsp	coriander powder
1 tsp	ginger-garlic paste
1	medium sized tomato (chopped)

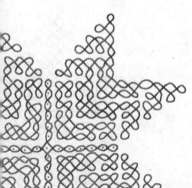

1. Clean the dal and pressure cook for 15 minutes along with turmeric powder and salt. The dal should be soft but the form retained.

2. Heat oil in a heavy vessel, and season with cloves and cinnamon. Add the onions and when transparent, add the dill leaves and fry till colour changes and the aroma of the dill emanates. Add chilli and coriander powder. Add ginger-garlic paste and chopped tomato. Fry and stir continuously till well blended. Add the cooked dal and stir fry. When the liquid evaporates and the whole curry becomes thick, remove from heat.

Serve with chapattis or with plain rice.

Serves 6

235

URULAKIZHANGU SOYIKEERAI VARIYAL

Fried Potatoes with Dill

500 gm	potatoes
4 tbsp	oil
1 tsp	mustard
1 tsp	split black gram dal
1	medium sized onion (chopped)
½ tsp	turmeric powder
3 tsp	coriander powder
2 tsp	chilli powder
¾ cup	finely chopped dill*
1 tsp	ginger-garlic paste
	Salt to taste

1. Boil the potatoes in their jackets, remove the skins and quarter them. Make sure that all the potato pieces are evenly sized.

2. Heat oil in an iron kadai, and season with mustard seeds, black gram dal. When the mustard splutters, add the onion, and the 3 powders and sauté for a minute. Add the dill, and sauté on low heat till it changes colour and the aroma emanates. Add the ginger-garlic paste and sauté till the whole is well blended. Add the potatoes and salt, and fry mixing the masala well, turning the potatoes over so that the masala covers them. Fry till all the liquid is absorbed, and sprinkle more water if the potatoes are not well coated. Add more oil if you feel that the potatoes are being scorched. Sauté till mixture becomes dry.

Serve with puris or chapattis or as a side dish with rice and curry.

Serves 6

* This dish can be done without dill. Tomatoes may be added if you don't like it so dry and curry leaves used instead of dill.

URULAKAZHANGU PUTTU

Potato Crumble

6 large	potatoes
4	green chillies

Seasoning

2 tbsp	oil
1 tsp	mustard seeds
1 tsp	split black gram dal
10	curry leaves
½ tsp	ginger-garlic paste
½ tsp	turmeric powder
¾ cup	water
	Salt to taste

To Garnish

¼ cup	chopped coriander leaves

1. Pressure cook the potatoes, and peel off the skin. Mash coarsely.

2. Finely chop onions and green chillies.

3. Heat oil in a kadai, and season with mustard seeds, split black gram dal and curry leaves. When it splutters, lightly brown onions and green chillies.

4. Add ginger-garlic paste and turmeric powder and fry for a few minutes.

5. Add ¾ cup water and salt to taste, and stir in potato mixture. Cook on low heat stirring well till water is absorbed and the mixture is dry.

6. Sprinkle coriander leaves, and mix well.

Note: *The potato puttu needs to be dry for masala dosai, but can be more liquid when served with puris.*

Makes about 50 puris

VAZHATHANDU KUTTU

Plantain Stem Curry with Lentils

Kuttu can be prepared with other vegetables such as brinjal, ridge gourd, snake gourd or bottle gourd. Green gram dal may be used instead of Bengal gram dal.

Plantain stem is believed to be a prophylactic and a remedy for stones in the gall bladder and kidney.

250 gm	plantain stem
1 cup	Bengal gram dal
¼ tsp	turmeric powder
¼ tsp	asafoetida
½ tsp	oil

To Grind

1 tsp	cummin seeds
4	green chillies
2 tbsp	grated coconut

Seasoning

2 tbsp	oil
1 tsp	mustard seeds
1 tsp	split black gram dal
20	curry leaves
4	red chillies (broken)
1	medium sized onion (chopped)
1	medium sized tomato
¼ cup	chopped coriander leaves

238

1. Chop the plantain stem into 1 inch cubes, and place in a vessel. Add enough water to cover it. Take a thin rough stick like a broom stick and swirl it around in the water. The fibre will twirl itself around the stick with the circular motion, and can be discarded.

2. Pressure cook the Bengal gram dal with turmeric powder, asafoetida and oil for 10 minutes. The dal should be soft, but its shape retained.

3. Grind the 3 ingredients listed.

4. Heat the oil in a heavy vessel and season with mustard seeds, black gram dal, curry leaves and red chillies. Add onions and when transparent, add the tomatoes, and sauté for a few minutes. Add the ground ingredients and the prepared plantain stem cubes and sauté for 3 minutes. Add the dal with the water and salt to taste, and simmer till the plantain stems cook. Add coriander leaves, mix well and remove from heat.

Serve with rice or chapattis.

Serves 5

UPPU THANI

Spinach Legume Curry

This is an exotic curry prepared from 4 different kinds of greens. The greens are described by their ethnic names, all of which are available in Tamil Nadu, but if they are not found elsewhere, other kinds of spinach may be successfully substituted. Suggested greens: Indian sorrel, red sorrel or Swiss chard. One small bunch is equivalent to 1 cup of leaves placed loosely in the cup without the stalks. Mochakka is another great favourite of Mudaliars in particular, and they belong to the family of legumes, closely resembling flat beans. They are shelled and then used, the skins are discarded.

1 small bunch	arrakeerai
1 small bunch	sirrukeerai
1 small bunch	molai keerai
1 small bunch	soyi keerai (dill)
250 gm	shelled mochakka
1	medium sized onion (chopped)
4 flakes	garlic
	Salt to taste

To Powder

1	cardamom
2	cloves
1	cinnamon

To Grind

½	coconut
2 tsp	poppy seeds

Seasoning

½ tsp	mustard seeds
½ tsp	split black gram dal
½ tsp	cummin seeds
1	medium sized onion
2	medium sized tomatoes
2 tsp	coriander powder
1 ½ tsp	chilli powder
½ tsp	turmeric powder
2 tsp	ginger-garlic paste
1	lime sized ball tamarind
1 tsp	ghee

1. Clean the greens, wash and chop fine. Add 1 cup of water and cook the greens along with salt, 1 chopped onion, and garlic flakes. Pressure cook the mochakka in ½ cup of water and salt. Grind ½ cup of cooked greens, and ½ cup of cooked mochakka without water.

2. Powder the spices listed and grind the coconut and the poppy seeds.

3. Heat oil and season with mustard seeds, black gram dal and cummin seeds. Add the chopped onion and when it becomes transparent, add tomatoes, and cook till they are well blended. Add the spice powder, the chilli, coriander and turmeric powders, the ginger -garlic paste, and fry till oil rises to the surface.

4. Add the ground coconut-poppy seed paste, the ground greens and mochakka, the rest of the cooked greens and mochakka, and the juice extracted from the tamarind. Let the gravy simmer on low heat for about 10 minutes. Add a teaspoon of ghee to enhance the flavour.

Serve hot with plain steamed rice.

Serves 7

VENDAKKAI VARUVAL

Fried Ladies Fingers

500 gm	ladies fingers
3 tbsp	oil
1 large	onion (chopped)
¼ tsp	turmeric powder
¾ tsp	coriander powder
½ tsp	chilli powder
	Salt to taste

1. Wash the ladies fingers. With a kitchen cloth wipe each to remove the fur. Snip off the ends. Slice into ½" pieces.

2. Heat the oil in a heavy kadai to smoking point and add chopped onions. Add the ladies fingers, and sauté till both are light brown. Add turmeric powder, coriander and chilli powder and salt. Mix the whole well, and sprinkle ¼ cup water. Cover and cook on low heat. When the vegetable is cooked and soft, continue to fry till dry.

Serve with sambhar and rice.

Serves 5

CARROT PUTTU

Carrot Crumble

250 gm	carrots
¼ tsp	turmeric powder
	Salt to taste

Seasoning

4 tsp	oil
2	cloves
½" piece	cinnamon
3	medium sized onions (finely chopped)
5	green chillies (finely chopped)
½ tsp	ginger-garlic paste

To Grind

¼	coconut
¼ cup	fried gram dal

To Garnish

¼ cup	chopped coriander leaves

1. Clean the carrots, scrape the skin off and grate finely. Add the turmeric and salt and 2 tablespoons of water and cook the grated carrot over high heat.
2. Heat oil in a kadai, and season with the whole spices. Add the onions and green chillies, frying till they are light brown in colour. Add the carrot with water if there is any and boil till water is completely absorbed.
3. Grind the coconut and the fried gram dal coarsely and add to the mixture, frying till the puttu turns golden brown.
4. Garnish with chopped coriander.

Serves 5

KARNAKAZHANGU VARUVAL

Fried Yam

500 gm	yam
¼ tsp	salt
¼ tsp	turmeric powder
3 tsp	coriander powder
2 tsp	chilli powder
1 dsp	thick tamarind extract
5 tbsp	oil

1. Apply oil on the hands, as handling the yam might cause itchiness. Slice off the skin of the yam, cut into half, and make ¼" thick slices. Apply turmeric powder and salt and pressure cook in half a cup of water for 5 minutes.

2. Make a thick paste of the coriander powder, chilli powder and tamarind extract. Taste a small piece of the yam and add extra salt if necessary to the paste. Smear the masala paste on to each piece evenly, both sides, and discard the water that the yam has been boiled in.

3. Heat 2 tablespoons of oil in a heavy griddle or tawa, and place 3 pieces at a time. Keeping the heat to medium, fry to a golden brown. When the oil has been absorbed add some more oil for the next batch as and when necessary.

Serve as accompaniment for any dal based curry but best with Moru Kozlambu.

Serves 6

Vegatables are used with great élan to create a wide range of tastes and flavours – ranging from sauted dishes to curry-based recipes.

1. Karnakazhangu
2. Vazha Thandu Pavakkai
3. Unshelled Mochakka
4. Kathrikkai
5. Kothrangai
6. Pavakhai
7. Vazhapoo
8. Poosinikkai

*Vegetarianism is increasingly being accepted
worldwide as the most healthy choice.*

1. Kuttu (Plantain Stem)
2. Keerai Poriyal (Sauted Greens)
3. Thayir Pachidi (Curd Salad)
4. Seppa Kazhangu Varuval (Fried Colocasia)

SEPPAKAZHANGU VARUVAL

Fried Colocacia

500 gm	colocasia (evenly sized)
½ tsp	turmeric powder
3 tsp	coriander powder
2 tsp	chilli powder
	Salt to taste
½ cup	oil
2 tblsp	rice flour

1. Wash the colocasia thoroughly to remove all sand and dirt. Boil till cooked. Each vegetable should be firm to touch and not overcooked. Remove the skins.

2. Cut each colocasia into 2, lengthwise. Smear the turmeric, coriander, chilli powders and salt evenly.

3. Heat 3 tablespoons of oil in a kadai, and add the prepared colocasia. Keep frying so that heat is distributed evenly. When it starts browning, add the rice flour, add more oil and fry. Add oil as necessary. You might need more oil than specified or less. When the colocasia has been roasted a golden brown, remove from heat.

Serve as accompaniment for a dal based dish.

Serves 6

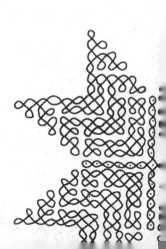

KATHRIKKAI VARUVAL

Stuffed Brinjal

500 gm	small round purple brinjals
1 tbp	oil

To Grind

1 tbsp	black pepper corns
1 tbsp	Bengal gram dal
4	red chillies
1 tsp	coriander seeds
1 tsp	cummin seeds
2	cloves
2 (1" piece)	cinnamon
1 large	onion
2 tsp	ginger-garlic paste
1	medium sized tomato
1	lime sized ball tamarind
	Salt to taste
¼ tsp	turmeric powder
4 tbsp	oil

To Garnish

½ cup	chopped coriander leaves

1. Wash the brinjals. Make criss-cross cuts leaving 2 inches of the stem intact. Set aside in a vessel of water.

2. Heat the oil in a kadai and sauté the first 7 ingredients listed under To Grind. Add the onions and fry till they are brown.

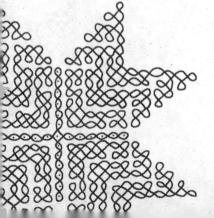

3. Remove from heat and add ginger-garlic paste, tomato and the tamarind, and mix the ingredients together, and grind to a smooth paste. Add salt and turmeric powder and mix well.

4. Stuff each brinjal with the ground masala. Any left over masala paste can be smeared over the vegetables.

5. Heat oil in an iron kadai and gently lower the stuffed brinjals into it. Sauté using a flat ladle to turn them over, till the brinjals are evenly brown and soft. Sprinkle half cup of hot water, cover and cook on low heat till the brinjals are done.

6. Garnish with chopped coriander leaves and serve with chapattis

Serves 6

VAZHAIPOO VADAI

Plantain Flower Patties

1	plantain flower
1 cup	Bengal gram (soak for 2 hours)
½ cup	grated coconut (grind to paste)

Powder individually

¾ cup	fried gram dal
1 tsp	cummin seeds
1" piece	cinnamon
3	cloves
2	medium sized onions (chopped fine)
6	green chillies (chopped fine)
1 cup	chopped coriander leaves
	Salt to taste
1 tsp	ghee
1 ½ cups	oil for frying

1. Remove the outer dark leaves encasing the plantain flower, and remove the flowers gently. Remove the stamen and the outer transparent pink skin at the base of each flower. Wash and clean the flowers, and boil them in water for about 3 minutes, taking care not to overcook them.

2. Grind the flowers to a coarse paste. Add all the other ingredients, mixing them smoothly. Add the ghee and mix.

3. Form into smooth lime sized balls, and flatten each in the hollow of your hand to form a vadai.

4. Deep fry the vadais in hot oil till they are golden brown. Drain the oil and lay it on kitchen paper so that all the excess oil is absorbed.

Serve hot with tomato sauce as a snack or at lunch time.

Serves 5

PAVAKKAI VARUVAL

Fried Bitter Gourd

250 gm	bitter gourd
	Salt to taste
1 ½ tsp	coriander powder
1 tsp	chilli powder
4 tbsp	oil

1. Snip off the ends of the bitter gourd. Slice thinly, smear with salt and set aside for half an hour. Squeeze out all the water and spread out on a plate. Smear with the turmeric powder, coriander and chilli powder.

2. Heat oil in a kadai, and add the bitter gourd. Fry on medium heat till it turns crisp and blackish brown in colour. This is best done on a tava where the vegatables can be spread out.

Serve as crispies along with a main meal.

Serves 6

R A S A M

*R*asams are thin soups which are eaten at the
end of a South Indian meal just before rounding
off with curds. It is supposed to act like a digestive
and no dyed -in-the. -wool Tamilian would consider
a meal complete without topping it off with the
good old rasam. Hot cooked rice is mashed with
the fingers, a few drops of ghee added, and hot
rasam poured over it and well blended. After a heavy
meal, you could take a cup of rasam instead of
having it with rice. Rasam could also be served as a
soup at the beginning of a meal. There are different
kinds of soups to suit each palate...

PARUPPU RASAM

Lentil Soup

¼ cup	red gram dal
4 flakes	garlic
1	pea sized piece asafoetida
½ tsp	oil
¼ tsp	turmeric powder
1	lime sized ball tamarind

Seasoning

1 tbsp	oil
1 tsp	ghee
1 tsp	mustard
¼ tsp	fenugreek
1	pea sized piece asoefatida
1 tsp	black gram dal
1 tsp	cummin seeds
10	curry leaves
5	red chillies(broken)
1 large	tomato (chopped fine)
1 tsp	jaggery
	Salt to taste
3 tbsp	chopped coriander leaves
1 sprig	curry leaves with stalk
4 flakes	garlic (with skin, and crushed)
2 heaped tsp	rasam powder (page 67)

1. Boil the dal with all the ingredients listed, and mash well.

2. The tamarind should be soaked for at least 2 hours, and the juice extracted.

3. Heat the oil and the ghee in a heavy vessel, and season with the ingredients listed. After the tomato is added, it should be fried till well blended and soft. Add 3 tablespoons of tamarind water and let it boil, so that the tomatoes are completely cooked. Add the rest of the tamarind water, and add 3 cups of water, the jaggery and salt to taste. Allow the liquid to boil for 5 minutes.

4. Add the dal along with the water. The rasam should be thinner than a curry, but thicker than a clear soup. When the rasam just begins to boil, add the pounded whole garlic with skin, the sprig of curry leaves and the coriander leaves. Switch off the heat and add the rasam powder, stir and cover with a lid. The rasam should never be allowed to boil after the dal is added.

Serve hot with rice and a teaspoon of ghee.

Serves 7

VERU RASAM

Tamarind Broth

1	lime sized ball tamarind
1	tomato

To Grind (coarsely)

5	red chillies
½ tsp	whole black pepper corns
1 tsp	cummin seeds
6 flakes	garlic
	Salt to taste

Seasoning

3 tsp	oil
1 tsp	mustard seeds
1 tsp	cummin seeds
3	pea sized pieces asafoetida
20	curry leaves
1 spring	coriander leaves (chopped)
4 flakes	garlic (with skin, and crushed)

1. The tamarind should be soaked for at least 2 hours. Remove the fibre and seeds and squeeze it in the water. Chop the tomato and add it to the tamarind and squeeze out the juice from both, retaining both the tamarind pith and the tomato skin in the vessel.

2. Coarsely grind the red chillies, whole black pepper, cummin seeds and garlic and mix into the tamarind water, adding water to make a thin liquid.

Add salt to taste. Place the rasam on heat and when it begins to boil, allow it to simmer for 6 minutes.

3. Meanwhile heat oil in a small pan and season with mustard seeds, asafoetida, cummin seeds and curry leaves. Add to the simmering rasam, keep on heat for a few minutes, and switch off the heat. Add the curry leaf sprig, the garlic and the green coriander, and close with a lid.

Serve hot with rice.

Serves 6

ELUMICHAPAZHAM RASAM

Lemon Broth

¼ cup	red gram dal
A pinch of	asafoetida powder
1 tsp	oil
¼ tsp	turmeric powder
1" piece	ginger
3	green chillies
½ tsp	cummin seeds
¾ tsp	pepper corns
2 tsp	oil
1 tsp	mustard seeds
2	red chillies (broken)
6	curry leaves
2	tomatoes (chopped)
	Salt to taste
1	lemon (extract juice)
2 tbsp	chopped coriander leaves

1. Pressure cook the dal with 1 cup of water, the turmeric and asafoetida powder, and 1 teaspoon of oil.

2. Grate the ginger and pound coarsely with the chopped green chillies. Broil the pepper corns and the cummin seeds and powder. Add these 4 ingredients to the cooked dal, and mix well.

3. Heat the oil in a kadai, and temper with mustard seeds, red chillies and curry leaves. Add chopped tomatoes and cook till soft.

4. Add dal mixture and bring to boil on low heat.

5. Turn off the heat, and add the lemon juice and garnish with chopped coriander.

Serve as a drink with meals or with hot rice.

Serves 6

KOLLU RASAM

Horsegram Soup

½ cup   horse gram

1. Soak the gram overnight, and pressure cook for 30 minutes the next morning in 3 cups of fresh water.

2. Follow the recipe for (Page 256). Grind half the quantity of cooked gram coarsely, and mix with the other ingredients which are ground for the , after which the recipe can be followed exactly. The water in which the gram has been cooked and the whole gram which has not been ground is to be added to the rasam before the seasoning.

Serve with hot rice or as a soup.

Serves 6

PICKLES

*P*ickles are part and parcel of a South Indian diet. Hot and spicy, they contribute that extra tang and fire, besides being aromatic. In my grandmother's day, the chilli powder was pounded at home using a giant mortar and pestle. The mortar was always made of stone, and the pounder of heavy seasoned wood with metal cladding at the edges. The women covered their nostrils and mouth to escape the fierce bite of the pungent chilli, as they pounded away in a pleasing rhythm.

The pickle season was at the height of summer when the sun sterilised the pickled fruit or vegetables. Mango and lime pickles are Tamilian favourites, while gooseberry and *narthangai* (belonging to the lime family) were used for certain disorders. Mouth-watering and tantalisingly red, and topped with pure oil, the pickle is eaten with curd rice, and one never goes without the other!

Absolute hygiene was the keyword for preserving the pickles for months, even a year. Women having their periods were forbidden to touch the pickle jar as it was believed that the pickles would spoil sooner!

NARTHANGA OORUKKAI

Bitter Orange Pickle

1 tbsp	oil
1	bitter orange
	A handful of salt
½ cup	chilli powder
¼ tsp	turmeric powder
1 tsp	fenugreek seeds
	(roasted and powdered)

Seasoning

1 cup	gingelly (sesame) oil
1 tsp	mustard seeds

1. Heat oil in a kadai and scald the bitter orange evenly. Allow it to cool and cut into 2" cubes.

2. Add the salt, chilli powder, turmeric powder and the powdered fenugreek to the narthangai and mix well.

3. Heat oil in a heavy vessel and season with mustard seeds. When it crackles, remove from heat, cool and add to the above. Use a wooden ladle to mix the ingredients, and shake the jar around so that the spices are evenly distributed.

Makes 150 gms

ELUMICHAPAZHAM OORUKKAI

Lime Pickle

8 cups	hot water
12	limes
½ tsp	turmeric powder
¾ cup	salt
½ cup	chilli powder

To Powder

1 tsp	fenugreek seeds
1	pea sized piece of asafoetida

Seasoning

¾ cup	gingelly (sesame) oil
2 tsp	mustard seeds
6	green chillies (slit)
1 pod	garlic (separated into flakes and skin removed)

1. Heat water to boiling point, add limes and turmeric powder. Remove from heat. Allow the limes to cool. Using a sharp knife, cut each lime into 8 pieces.

2. Powder the salt if you are using rock salt and add to the limes. Place them in a porcelain pickle jar, and shake the jar so that the salt is evenly mixed. Cover with a lid and allow to rest for 24 hours.

3. The next day, shake the jar around, so that the salt is evenly distributed. Add chilli powder and mix evenly using a wooden ladle which is absolutely clean and dry.

4. Dry roast the fenugreek seeds, and fry the asafoetida in a little oil. Powder these 2 ingredients, and add to the limes.

5. Heat the oil in a heavy vessel, and season with mustard seeds, green chillies and garlic. The chillies and the garlic are optional, and the pickles may be done without them. When the seasoning crackles, switch off the heat and allow the oil to cool to room temperature.

6. Add the oil with the seasoning to the pickles. Close the mouth of the jar. Sun the pickles every 2 weeks, removing the lid, and covering the mouth of the jar with a clean muslin cloth. Make sure that the oil covers the pickle. If not you can top it with extra oil for better preservation.

Makes 200 - 250 gms

MANGA OORUKKAI

Mango Pickle

12	large mangoes

To Powder

2 tbsp	mustard
1 tbsp	fenugreek seeds

½ tsp	asafoetida powder
3 cups	chilli powder
2 tbsp	turmeric powder
3 cups	salt

Seasoning

3 cups	gingelly (sesame) oil
1 tsp	mustard seeds

1. Wash the mangoes, wipe dry with a clean cloth and sun dry for 3-4 hours. Chop each mango into 2" cubes along with the seed, and store in a clean pickle jar.

2. Roast the mustard and fenugreek seeds and powder fine. Add chilli powder, turmeric powder, asafoetida and salt and mix all the ingredients well. Add the powder to the mango pieces, and mix the whole using a flat wooden ladle.

3. Heat the oil to smoking point, and season with mustard seeds. When they crackle, remove from heat and allow to cool. Pour the oil with the seasoning over the mango pieces, and stir the contents with the wooden ladle.

4. Sun dry the pickles every 2 weeks.

Makes 1 kg

MANGA INJI OORUKKAI

Mango-Ginger Pickle

Mangai inji *is a root vegetable which is part of the ginger family with the smell and taste of mango.*

250 gms	mangai inji (ginger)
2 cups	oil
2 tsp	mustard seeds
½ tsp	fenugreek seeds
2 pods	garlic (pounded coarsely)
25 gms	chilli powder
½ tsp	turmeric powder
½ cup	salt
25 gms	tamarind (soaked and juice extracted)

1. Finely chop the ginger.

2. Heat the oil in a heavy vessel, and season with mustard and fenugreek seeds. When they splutter, add chopped ginger and fry for 2-3 minutes. Add pounded garlic and sauté for a minute. Add chilli powder, turmeric powder and salt, and fry till oil rises to the surface.

3. Add thick extract of tamarind and simmer for 5-7 minutes.

4. Cool and store in clean glass jars and refrigerate.

If the pickles are to be consumed withing a short period of time, the amount of oil and salt may be reduced.

Makes 400 gms

MANGA THOKKU

Grated Mango Pickle

4 cups	green sour mangoes (grated)
½ cup	gingelly (sesame) oil
¾ cup	chilli powder
¼ tsp	turmeric powder
½ tbsp	fenugreek seeds (roasted and powdered)
¼ tsp	asafoetida
½ cup	salt

1. Clean the mangoes, peel and grate.

2. Heat oil in a kadai and and fry the grated mangoes. Add chilli powder, turmeric powder, fenugreek powder, asafoetida and salt. Stir till the oil leaves the sides of the vessel.

3. Remove from heat, cool and store in an air tight porcelain jar.

Makes 300 gms

NELLIKKAI OORUKKAI

Gooseberry Pickle

3 cups	gooseberries
1 cup	oil
2 tsp	mustard seeds
¼ cup	curry leaves
½ tsp	asafoetida
½ cup	chilli powder
¼ tsp	turmeric powder
1 tsp	fenugreek seeds (roasted and powdered)
½ cup	salt

1. Boil water in a vessel and add the gooseberries. Cook till tender and set aside to cool.

2. Heat oil in a kadai, season with mustard seeds. When they crackle, lower heat, add curry leaves, asafoetida, chilli and turmeric powder, and fenugreek powder. Add the gooseberries and sauté for a few minutes. Add the salt and stir, mixing all the ingredients.

3. Cool and store in a clean jar. This pickle preserves better when refrigerated.

Makes 300 gms

KOTHAMALLI OORUKKAI

Green Coriander Pickle

2 large bunches	fresh tender coriander
2" piece	ginger
2 pods	garlic
1 cup	oil
1 tsp	mustard seeds
½ tsp	fenugreek seeds
50 gms	chilli powder
½ tsp	turmeric powder
25 gms	tamarind (soaked and juice extracted)
½ cup	Salt

1. Wash the coriander leaves with the tender stalks, and chop very fine.

2. Scrape the skin off the ginger, chop into small pieces. Remove the skins from the garlic flakes, and pound both together coarsely.

3. Heat oil in a kadai, and season with mustard and fenugreek seeds. When they crackle, add chopped coriander and fry for 5 minutes, stirring continuously. Add the ginger-garlic paste, followed by chilli and turmeric powder. Sauté till oil rises to the surface.

4. Add tamarind extract and salt and fry for a few minutes.

5. Cool and store in a clean glass bottle. Refrigerate if you wish to preserve it longer.

The quantity of salt and oil may be reduced for immediate consumption.

Makes 200 gms

SWEETS

*S*weets, as they are called, are prepared for all auspicious occasions and on festival days. They are served at marriages and at functions. The Tamilian will serve the sweet first, before the main meal, as one is supposed to sweeten one's tongue before partaking of any food. Payasam, which is a thin or thick milk based drink, is considered very special during the many festivals of the Tamils. Many of the sweets like laddus and burfis can be made and stored in airtight tins, while some others need to be consumed quickly.

PAAL PAYASAM

Milk Payasam

75 gm	long grain rice
A few strands	saffron
1 tbsp	warm milk
750 ml	milk
1 cup	water
4 heaped tbsp	sugar
½ tsp	ground cardamom

To Garnish

Thin slices	almonds

1. Wash the rice and spread out to dry on a paper or cloth. Pound to break the grains coarsely.

2. Soak the saffron strands in the warm milk.

3. In a heavy, large pan, boil the milk over moderate heat, stirring all the time so that it does not get burnt. Boil for about 40 minutes, till the milk thickens and is reduced by half. Add the rice and the water, and boil till the rice is cooked. Add the sugar, cardamom and saffron-milk, stir and simmer for 10 minutes till the sugar dissolves.

4. Serve in glasses or bowls and garnish with sliced almonds.

Serves 6

272

SEMIYA PAYASAM

Vermicelli Payasam

1 cup	broken vermicelli
½ lt	hot water
2 cups	milk
1 cup	sugar
A pinch of	salt
A few strands	saffron
1 tbsp	warm milk
1 tbsp	ghee
20 gm	cashew nuts
10 gm	raisins
½ tsp	powdered cardamom

1. Soak the strands of saffron in the warm milk. Broil the vermicelli in a heavy bottomed vessel till it changes colour lightly. Take care that it does not become too brown. Gradually pour the hot water over it, stirring constantly and gently so that no lumps are formed. Keep on heat till the vermicelli is cooked and is soft to touch. Add the milk, stir till it comes to the boil. Add sugar and salt, stir, and let the whole boil till the sugar dissolves. Set aside.

2. Heat the ghee in a pan, and fry 10 grams of split cashew nuts, and all the raisins.

3. Powder the remaining cashew nuts, add to the payasam along with the fried cashew nuts and raisins, and the saffron milk, and let the payasam simmer for a minute. Cool and serve in tumblers.

Serves 6

RAVA KESRI

Semolina Sweet

¾ cup	ghee
10	cashew nuts
¼ cup	chopped cashew nuts
1 ½ tbsp	raisins
2 cups	semolina
1 ¾ cups	very hot water
2 cups	sugar
¼ tsp	powdered cardamom
A few strands	saffron
¼ tsp	saffron powder

1. Split the 10 cashew nuts into halves, and lightly brown them in 2 teaspoons of ghee, along with the raisins and set aside in another vesel for garnishing.

2. In the same vessel add the rest of the ghee, and fry the semolina till light brown. Add the hot water and stir on heat till semolina is cooked and becomes soft. Add sugar and rest of the spices, and keep on medium heat till all the ingredients are well blended.

Spread on a plate and garnish with fried cashewnuts and raisins. Can be served hot or cold.

Serves 6

THITHEEPU PONGAL

Sweet Rice

This sweet is offered to the sun god on the day of Pongal or the harvest festival, which is an important one in South India, especially to agriculturists. A new mud pot is placed in the sun and the pongal cooked in it. After the dal and rice are cooked, the milk is poured in. When it boils over the pot in one foamy trail, there is great excitement, and young children of the family dance around the pot with cries of "Pongalo Pongal!"

1 cup	raw rice
½ cup	green gram dal
½ tsp	salt
3 cups	powdered jaggery
1 ½ cups	milk
4 tbsp	ghee
2 tbsp	cashew nuts
3 tbsp	raisins
3	cardamoms (pounded)
½	nutmeg (grated)

1. Clean and wash the rice. Clean the dal, dry roast and wash. Pressure cook both together for 10 minutes in 4 cups of water adding salt.

2. Mix the jaggery with 1 cup of water and cook on low heat till the jaggery dissoves. Strain the liquid using a muslin cloth, to remove impurities. Add to the dal and rice. Add the milk and cook till absorbed. The mixture should not be too dry, nor too liquid, but a soft mixture of cooked dal and rice.

3. Heat ghee in a small pan and add cashew nuts and raisins. Stir this into the pongal. Add the cardamom and the nutmeg and mix thoroughly with the pongal.

Serve hot.

Serves 5

THITHEEPU APPAM

Sweet Steamed Pancakes

1 litre	raw rice
100 gms	black gram dal
1 large	coconut
6	cardamoms
4	bananas (poovam pazham)
750 gms	powdered jaggery
½ tsp	saffron powder
50 gms	soda-bicarbonate
	Ghee for frying

1. Soak the rice and dal in water for 1 hour. Drain and grind along with grated coconut and cardamom. Add bananas and powdered jaggery, grind well and set aside. Dissolve the saffron powder mixed in a little water, and add to the dough, stirring well to absorb it evenly.

2. Just before pouring out the appams, soda-bicarbonate is mixed with a little water and added to the dough.

3. Heat an iron griddle or tawa, and pour 1 deep ladleful of dough, spreading it evenly but keeping it thick. Pour 2 teaspoons of ghee round it, and let it cook. Flip over the other side and allow to cook. Cut into wedges and serve.

Serves 5

*An enticing variety of spices are employed with imagination
to create the traditional dishes of the South.*

Tamilians serve the sweet first to sweeten the tongue before partaking of the main meal.

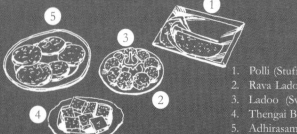

1. Polli (Stuffed Sweet Bread)
2. Rava Ladoo (Semolina Balls)
3. Ladoo (Sweet Lentil Flour Balls)
4. Thengai Burfi (Coconut Sweet)
5. Adhirasam (Jaggery and Rice Flour Cakes)

LADOO

Sweet Lentil Flour Balls

2 ½ cups	sugar
2 ½ cups	water
A few strands	saffron
4	cardamoms (powdered)
2 ½ cups	Bengal gram flour
1 ½ cups	oil
2 tbsp	ghee
10	cashew nuts
14	raisins

1. Make a thin syrup with the sugar and water, which would be a one thread consistency. Remove the scum from the surface with a spoon. Remove from heat and add saffron and powdered cardamom.

2. Make a thick dropping batter by adding water to the gram flour.

3. Heat the oil in a kadai. Place a large flat spoon with pepper sized holes, and drop one ladle of batter on to it. Fry these little droplets of batter *(boondi)* till golden brown. Repeat the process till all the batter is used. Add the boondi to the sugar syrup.

4. Fry the cashew nuts and raisins in the ghee and add to the the laddu mixture. Mix thoroughly and form into small balls, the size of large lemons. The mixture should be compressed with the palms of the hands, and made into balls. Place on a large plate to cool, after which they can be stored in airtight tins.

Makes about 20 laddoos

KADLAKKAI URUNDAI

Peanut Balls

2 cups	broken peanuts
2 cups	powdered jaggery
1 cup	water
¼ cup	ghee
1 tbsp	rice flour

1. Dry roast the coarsely broken nuts.

2. Prepare a thick syrup with the jaggery and water, of two thread consistency. Add the ghee, and when evenly distributed, remove from heat. Stir in peanuts, and mix well. Smear the palms and fingers of your hands with rice flour, and scoop up the peanut mixture and shape into lemon sized balls. Allow to cool and harden.

Store in airtight tins.

Makes about 15-20 cookies

THENGAI BURFI

Coconut Sweet

2 cups	sugar
2 cups	water
2 cups	grated coconut
A few drops	colouring
½ cup	ghee
¼ cup	chopped cashew nuts
¼ tsp	powdered cardamom

1. Make a thin syrup with the sugar and water, which would be a one thread consistency. Remove the scum from the surface with a spoon.

2. Add the grated coconut and stir well till it thickens. Add the colouring of your choice. Add ghee and the cashew nuts and cardamom powder. Mix well. When the ghee starts coming out of the mixture, and when it begins to leave the sides, turn over on to a greased plate, and press down evenly. Mark into diamonds and cut before fully set.

Makes about 20 sweets

KOZHAKATTAI

Rice Flour Cookies

This sweet is used as an offering during the Ganesh festival, as this favourite deity is supposed to love it.

Filing

1½ cups	white sesame seeds
6	cardamoms (skinned and pounded)
1 cup	powdered jaggery
2 cups	rice
2 cups	water
A pinch of	salt
1 tsp	sesame oil

1. Wash the sesame seeds a number of times till the water turns clear. Soak for 1 hour. Drain the water and spread the seeds on a clean white cloth. When nearly dry, pound it to a fairly coarse powder. Mix with the powdered cardamom and jaggery and set aside.

2. Clean and wash the rice and soak for 3 hours. Drain the water and spread out on a clean white cloth to dry. When half damp (the rice should not dry out fully), grind to a powder in a mixie. Sift it using a fine sieve.*

3. Boil 2 cups of water with the pinch of salt and sesame oil. Gradually add the rice flour, and stir vigorously with a wooden spoon, ensuring that no lumps have formed, and the water is fully absorbed. Place the dough in a vessel and cover with a damp muslin cloth so that it does not dry out.

4. When the dough cools sufficiently, knead it with your hand making a smooth, soft, pliable dough. Grease a square of plastic, or banana leaf, or the palm of your hand whichever is convenient to you, and press down a lime sized ball of dough to make a thin circle, about 4 inches in diameter. Place a teaspoon of filling in the centre of the circle. Dampen one half of the edge, and bring the other over to close it pressing the edges down with the fingers, to seal it. Use a wheel cutter to trim the edges.

5. The kozhakattais are steamed for 7-10 minutes and served when cool. The filling can have variations according to taste.* *

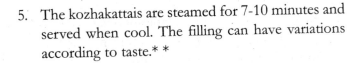

* Steam sieved flour for 7 minutes, then immediately sift again rubbing lumps on sieve. This makes the flour soft.

** 1 cup grated coconut and ¾ cup powdered jaggery can be used as an alternate filling. Add a tablespoon of water to the jaggery and stir on moderate heat till the jaggery dissolves and begins to boil. Remove scum and allow the syrup to thicken. Add the coconut scrapings, continue stirring on low heat till water is absorbed. Remove from heat and add 5 powdered cardamoms. Make the kozhakattais in the same way, using this filling.

Makes 20 cookies

RAVA LADDOO

Semolina Balls

½ cup	ghee
1 ½ cups	semolina
1 ½ cups	sugar
6	cardamoms
¼ cup	cashew nuts
¼ cup	raisins

1. Roast the semolina in 2 tablespoons ghee or more if required. The semolina should not brown too much, but should turn light brown.

2. Powder the sugar, skinned cardamoms and the semolina in a mixer.

3. Heat the remaining ghee and fry the cashew nuts and raisins. Add to the semolina and sugar. Form into small lime sized balls, compressing each tightly. Cool and store in airtight tins. Being quite fragile, they have to be handled carefully.

Makes 15 laddoos

POLLI

Stuffed Sweet Bread

1 cup	Bengal gram dal
1 cup	powdered jaggery
7	cardamoms
1 heaped cup	refined flour
1 tsp	powdered sugar
¼ tsp	turmeric powder
¼ cup	ghee

1. Clean and cook the dal till soft, and drain the excess water. Add jaggery and cardamoms and cook on low heat till the jaggery has dissolved and the moisture absorbed. Grind to a smooth paste without adding water.

2. Mix the rest of the ingredients and make a soft pliable dough using a little water to knead it. Make lime sized balls. Grease your palm and press each ball against it, flattening it into a round of 3" diameter. Place 2 teaspoons of filling and bring one edge of the circle to cover the other, pressing the edges to seal them completely. Dust a square piece of muslin with refined flour, and press each filled dough piece into a round of 6" diameter.

3. Fry each polli on a tawa or griddle with a teaspoon of ghee poured round the edges till light brown. Flip over the other side and brown, and cook all the pollis similarly.

Makes 15

ADHIRASAM

Jaggery and Rice Flour Cakes

Adhirasams are a Deepavali speciality, and a must for every Tamilian household. A specific number of adhirasams are made for Varalakshmi Nombu which is celebrated on the day after Deepavali. This festival is observed with reverance by married women for the good of their husbands and families.

250 gms	fine quality raw rice
1 tsp	powdered dry ginger
4	cardamom (powdered)
200 gm	powdered jaggery
½ cup	water
1 ½ cups	refined oil

1. Clean the rice and wash it. Soak the rice for 3-4 hours. Drain the water and spread the rice out to dry on a white cloth. When the rice is still damp, powder fine in a mixie. Add ginger powder and cardamom powder and mix well. Pass the powder through a fine sieve.

2. Add water to the jaggery in a heavy bottomed vessel and allow to boil. Remove the scum from the jaggery using a ladle. Make a syrup of soft ball consistency. Add the flour gradually, mixing vigorously till it is completely added. Remove from heat and continue stirring till the dough thickens. Cover the mouth of the vessel with a damp muslin cloth.

3.   Heat the oil in a kadai. Take a lime sized ball of dough and flatten it into a small round about 4" in diameter, on a greased banana leaf or a small plastic sheet. Gently ease the adhirasam into the oil, and when browned, turn over to brown the other side. Place the adhirasam on a perforated plate placed on another plate, and press down with a flat plate to remove the excess oil, which is collected in the bottom most plate. This oil can be poured back into the kadai. Repeat the process till all the athirasams are done. These can be stored up to a month in an airtight container.

Note: *It is always advisable to keep some extra rice flour in case the dough becomes too sticky and therefore unmanageable.*

Makes 25

DIAMOND GAJUR

Rice Flour Pastries

250 gm	refined flour
A pinch of	salt
200 gm	rice flour
50 gm	ghee
1 ½ cups	oil

1. Sift the refined flour and add salt. Knead with water to make a soft pliable dough. Cover and set aside for 1 hour.

2. Mix the rice flour and ghee with the fingertips to form a smooth paste.

3. Take a lime sized ball of the dough, and roll out into a thin circle. Smear the rice flour paste over the surface, and cover with another thin dough circle. Using a rolling pin, flatten these two sand-wiched circles, into a thin large square. Use a cutter wheel to cut into diamonds, about 2 ½"-3" in length.

4. Pour the oil into a kadai and deep fry the diamonds to a golden brown. Dust with castor sugar coating both sides, cool and store in airtight tins.

Note: *Savoury gajoors may be made by kneading salt with the dough, and omitting the sugar altogether.*

Makes 35-40

PUZHUNGAL ARISI HALWA

Parboiled Rice Cookies

1 cup	boiled rice
1 large	coconut
2 cups	sugar
5	cardamoms (crushed)
1 cup	ghee
2 tbsp	poppy seeds

1. Soak boiled rice for 2 hours or more. Drain water and grind to a fine paste.

2. Grate the coconut and extract the milk. Add to rice paste and mix.

3. Boil sugar with 1½ cups of water. Remove the scum, and simmer till a soft ball consistency is reached. Add the rice paste and cardamom. Stir till the mixture thickens and add ghee gradually, till the halwa leaves the sides of the vessel.

4. Pour the mixture into a greased plate, and cut into squares when nearly cool.

Makes 50 squares of 1½" each

THITHEEPU VADAI

Lentil Doughnuts

250 gms	black gram dal
50 gms	powdered jaggery
1 ripe	plantain (mashed)
1 tsp	ghee
1 ½ cups	oil (for deep frying)

1. Clean the dal, and soak for 2 hours. Drain the water completely, and grind to a smooth paste without adding water. Add the jaggery and the plantain and grind together. Water should be avoided as the addition of jaggery will make the dough runny. Add ghee, and mix well.

2. Heat oil to smoking point in a heavy kadai.

3. Wet your hands, take a small lime sized ball of dough and pat it into a thick round on a small square of plastic or a banana leaf. Make a hole in the centre with your finger, and gently slide it into the hot oil. Fry on both sides to a rich brown colour.

Serve hot or cold.

Note: *Keep a small bowl of cold water beside you. Dip your fingers into it each time you feel that the dough adheres to your hand. This helps form the vadais, and besides, you can slide it off the leaf or plastic more easily.*

Makes 30

MUTTAI HALWA

Egg Cookies

6	eggs
½ loaf	bread
250 gm	castor sugar
3 gm	saffron strands
15	almonds (shelled, and ground to a paste)
200 gm	ghee
50 gm	raisins

1. Break the eggs into a bowl and beat lightly.

2. Remove the crust from the bread, slice, and soak in water for 15 minutes. Squeeze out the water and mash the bread.

3. Add the bread, sugar, saffron strands and almond paste to the eggs, and blend in a mixie, till the consistency is smooth.

4. Place a heavy vessel over moderate heat, and melt the ghee. Add the raisins and sauté till they puff up. Add the liquidised ingredients, and stir. As soon as the halwa reaches boiling point, lower the heat, and continue to stir till the halwa leaves the sides of the vessel.

The halwa should be ready in an hour's time, and is best served hot.

Serves 6

CALORIE CHART

Food categories	Measure	Calories
MILK PRODUCTS		
Whole milk	1 cup	150
Whole milk yoghurt	1 cup	150
Ghee	1 tbsp	45
CEREAL		
Cooked rice	½ cup	80
Chapatti	1 medium	80
STARCHY VEGETABLES		
Potato	1 medium	80
Pumpkin	¾ cup	80
Cooked dal	1 cup	80
Plantain	½ cup	80
Mixed vegetables	⅔ cup	80
MEAT		
Lean goat meat or boneless chicken	1 serving (40-50 gm)	55
FISH	50 gm	55
MEDIUM FAT		
Mutton 1 serving	(40 gm)	75
Egg	1	75
Liver, kidney	1 serving (40 gm)	75
Deep fried meat	1 serving	100

Food categories	Measure	Calories
SNACKS		
Plain dosai	1 medium	135
Masala dosai	1 medium	250
s	6 (50 gm)	175
	1 large	85
Samosa	1 piece	140
Vadai	1	70
MAIN DISHES		
Mutton biriyani	1 cup	225
Vegetable biriyani	1 cup	200
Chicken curry	1 serving	200
Fish curry with coconut	1 serving	250
Mutton curry	1 serving	225
Vegetable curry	1 serving	135

1 serving of each curry
would be approximately 100 gm.

Fried chicken	1 piece(50 gm)	120
Fried fish	1 piece (85 gm)	140
Potato varaiyal	100 gm	145
Chicken soup	1 cup	120
Vegetable soup	1 cup	80
SWEETS		
Halwas	1 piece(45 gm)	165
Ladoo	1 small piece (30 gm)	175
Payasam	100 gm	180

This is a generalised calorie chart of some of the main dishes or ingredients mentioned in the book. Calories correspondingly of other dishes can be easily worked out using the above as a guideline. The chart is given to help the calorie conscious to work out a sensible diet.

SPECIAL
MENUS

*I*f you wish to serve traditional Tamil Nadu food
for your guests, here are some menus which I found
are greatly appreciated whenever we have entertained.
Mixing and matching are prerogatives of the hostess,
but the old time combinations were remarkably well
adjusted in terms of nutrition, flavour, texture and
colour, complementing one another so well, that it was
difficult to eat one dish without the other!

Menu 1

Mutton Biriyani
Brinjal curry (Yennai kathrikkai kozhambu)
Fried fish slices
Tomato pachidi
s
Fried potatoes with dill
 (to be served as a soup)
Curd
Lime pickle
Diamond gajur

Menu 2

Semolina uppumav
Stuffed snake gourd curry
   (vegetarian or non-vegetarian)
Cucumber salad
Chapattis
Fried ladies fingers
Ulutham vadai
Curd rice
Mango pickle
Pappad
Ladoos
Vermicelli payasam

Menu 3

Coconut rice
Meat ball currry (Mudaliar)
Mint pachidi
Egg fry
White rice
Thayir vadai

Paruppu rasam
Greens in tamarind sauce
Appalam
Kothimalli pickle

Menu 4

Chapatti
Spinach curry
Kyma vadais or Plantain flower vadais
Puliyodorai
Potato puttu
White rice
Narthangai pickle
Paruppu rasam

Menu 5

Appam
Aattu kaal kozhambu
Fish curry
Tomato rice
Onion salad
Carrot puttu
Colocasia fry
Kollu rasam
Grated mango pickle
Rava kesari

GLOSSARY
OF
INGREDIENTS

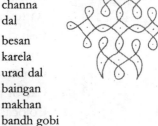

English	Tamil	Hindi
almond	baadaam	badam
amaranth leaves	molai keerai	cholai-ka-saag
aniseed	sombu	saunf
asoefatida	peringayam	hing
banana	vazha pazham	kela
bay leaves	brinj illai	tej patta
beans	beans	seem
bengal gram	dal	channa
	kadalai paruppu	dal
Bengal gram flour	kadalai mavu	besan
bitter gourd	pavakkai	karela
black gram dal	ulutham paruppu	urad dal
brinjal or aubergine	kathrikkai	baingan
butter	vennai	makhan
cabbage	muttai ghos	bandh gobi
capsicum or		
green pepper	koda milagai	simla mirch
cardanom	ellakkai	elaichi
carrot	carrot	gajjar
cauliflower	cauliflower	phool gobi
chick peas	mooku kadalai	kabuli chana
chilli (green)	pachai milagai	hara mirch
chilli (red)	kaanja milagai	lal mirch
chow chow	seemai kathrikkai	chow chow
cinnamon	pattai	dal chini
cloves	lavangam	lavang

298

English	Tamil	Hindi
coconut	thengai	nariyal
colocasia	seppa kizhangu	arvi
copra	coprai	copra
coriander leaves/		
cilanthro	kothimalli	hara dhania
coriander seeds	dhania	dhania
cucumber	vellarikka	
	or keerakkai	kheera
cummin seeds	seeragam	zeera
curds	thayir	dahi
curry leaves	karivepilai	kari patha
dill (green, fresh)	soyikeerai	soyi ki bhajji
dry ginger	chukku	saunth
drumsticks	murungakkai	sajjan
fenugreek seeds	vendhiyam	methi
fenugreek leaves	vendhikeerai	methi ki bhajji
fried gram dal	pottu kadalai	bhuna chana
garlic		lahsun
gherkins	kovakkai	kundru
gingelly	ellu	til
ginger	inji	adhrak
green gram dal	pachai paruppu	moong dal
	or paithiyam paruppu	
ground nut	ver kadalai	moongphali
jaggery	vellam	gur
kohl rabi	knol kol	knol kol
ladies fingers or		
okra	vendakkai	bhindi
lime/lemon	elumichapazham	nimbu
mango (raw)	mangai	aam
mango (ripe)	mampazham	aam
milk	paal	doodh
mint	pudina	pudina
mustard seeds	kadigu	rai
nutmeg	jadikkai	jaiphal
onion	vengayam	pyaaz
shallots	sambhar	
	vengayam	pyaaz
parboiled rice	puzhungal arisi	usna chaval
peas	pattani	mattar
peanuts	ver kadalai	moongphali
peppercorns (black)	milagu	kali mirch
poppy seeds	khuskhusa	khuskhus

English	Tamil	Hindi
potato	urulakazhangu	aloo
radish	mulangi	mooli
ragi	kevaru	madua
raisins	dratchi	kismis
red gram dal	tuvaram paruppu	tooar dal
refined flour	maida mavu	maida
rice	arisi	chawal
ridge gourd	peerkangai	torai
saffron	kungumapoo	kesar
sago	javarasi	sabudana
salt	uppu	namak
semolina	ravai	rava or sooji
snake gourd	podalangai	chachinda
sugar	chakkarai	cheeni
sugar syrup	chakkarai pavu	sheera
tamarind	puli	imli
tapioca	mara velli kizhangu	simla aloo
tomato	thakkali	tamatar
turmeric	manjal	haldi
vermicelli	semiya	seviyan
wheat	godumai	gehoon
whole wheat flour	godumai mavu	atta
yam	chenai kizhangu	jimikand or sooran

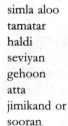

COOKING TERMS

Batter   To form a thick paste which is pourable.

Beat   To incorporate air as you process the ingredients either with an electric mixer or a fork.

Blanch   To place an ingredient in boiling water for a minute to soften the skin for easy removal.

Blend   When two or more ingredients are so thoroughly mixed that they are incorporated to form a smooth integrated whole.

Broil   To fry the ingredients in a tawa without oil, browning them.

Chop   To cut the ingredients in small or large pieces.

Consistency   Thickness of the mixture.

Colander   A vessel having small holes, used to strain liquids.

Dough   A mixture of flour and liquid mixed till soft and not sticky.

Dry roast	Same as broil.
Grate	To shred a vegetable by rubbing against the holes in a grater.
Kadai	An iron vessel with a round bottom, like a wok.
Knead	To work the dough with the hands, pummelling it till the dough becomes soft and pliable.
Marinate	To soak the ingredients in lime juice, curds or vinegar to soften the vegetable or meat.
Saute	To stir in oil.
Sift	To pass ingredients through a sieve.
Simmer	To boil on low heat.
Shred	To cut ingredients in thin long strips with a knife or shredder.
Stir	To mix with a ladle using a rotary action.
Tawa	A flat iron griddle.

NOTES

Tamarind is used in a number of recipes in this book. Whenever a recipe calls for tamarind, soak the specified quantity in water before you start assembling your other ingredients. Tamarind becomes soft when soaked for 2 hours. Squeeze it with your fingers, strain the extract into another vessel. Add a small quantity of water to remove the residual juice. Discard the pith and seeds.

Coconut milk is effectively extracted when warm water is poured over the grated coconut. It can be manually extracted by using your fingers in the same way as for tamarind. Your work is reduced if you use a liquidiser, in which case warm water is not necessary.

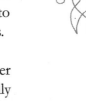

Seasoning imparts a delicate flavour to the dish. The oil should never be overheated, nor the seasoning left too long in the oil before the other ingredients are added. As in the case of mustard and dal, you should wait for the mustard seeds to burst before you add the onions. Season with whole spices means seasoning with cinnamon, cloves and cardamom.

Vadagam adds a special taste to the curry. The making of this seasoning is somewhat tedious, but the next best thing is substituting 1 teaspoon of *vadagam* with ½ teaspoon mustard seeds, ½ teaspoon black gram dal, ¼ teaspoon fenugreek and 8 curry leaves.

Peeled garlic may be refrigerated which makes usage convenient. For easy peeling, smear the garlic with oil and place under strong sunlight. Rub it on a rough surface and hey presto, much of the drudgery is eliminated.

Whenever time permits, grind **garlic and ginger** separately and store in small glass jars or plastic containers in the refrigerator. It helps whenever you need to do a spot of hurried cooking.

I always keep **mixed chilli powder,** again to cut down on extra work. Red chillies and dry coriander in the proportion 1:1 1/2 are dried in the sun or oven dried, and ground to a fine powder, and stored for one or two months in an airtight container.

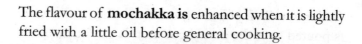

The flavour of **mochakka is** enhanced when it is lightly fried with a little oil before general cooking.

The **pressure cooker** cuts down the tedium of long hours in the kitchen. The time calculated for the cooking is from the moment the pressure cooker lets out a loud hiss. For instance, if a recipe calls for meat to be pressure cooked for 15 minutes, it means you switch off the stove 15 minutes after the pressure is reached, when the pressure cooker lets out a loud hiss.

INDEX

307

Acknowledgements

I gratefully acknowledge the help of friends and family particularly my mother – Leela Chander, Seetha Muthiah Venila Thiagarajan, Mahema & Manohar Devadoss for sharing their recipes – Ram Gopala krishnan for his unstinted support throughout, helping with the computer, the prinouts and drawings.

About the Author

I belong to a Tamilian community where food is rated very high. Born and brought up in Bangalore and living in a family which observed convention as well as some principles of modernity, I learnt to respect food as being something precious, and definitely not to be wasted. I still have childhood memories of the number of people my parents hosted, the way they sat round our huge dining table, and how my father discussed the day's menu with my mother. As children we loved to ride with my father to Rusell Market for groceries, vegetables and meat for those special family get-togethers while the rest of the city slept. I remember the mounds of the family's favourite beans... *mochakka,* during the winter season.

Coffee making was an art... the coffee seeds were roasted and ground at home, to make just enough powder for the day. I can still close my eyes and recall the aroma of coffee being made in the coffee-filters, even though it was a banned drink for us as children!

My father, who was a doctor, did not believe in refrigeration. Cooked food was eaten piping hot and leftovers distributed to the hungry. Fresh food was always cooked in the evening for the night meal. Excepting my mother, our family was non-vegetarian, and my father personally shopped for the best of meat, chicken and fish. Cooking intrigued me, and I was fascinated at the amount of effort it took to produce a good meal. Early marriage and moving away from home prevented me from learning first-hand traditional receipes from my mother, though of course, she sent me recipes regularly by post, to far-away Bhopal where my husband and I lived. But the inputs I received as I grew up, remained with me through my adult life.

My inspiration to becoming a good cook was my husband, who apart from being an engineer has remarkable prowess in innovating and creating his own recipes. The exotic *chuppal* curry in this book is a 60-year-old speciality from his family, inspired by Persian friends and their cuisine. It was a challenge for me to keep up the family tradition of

Acknowledgements

I gratefully acknowledge the help of friends and family particularly my mother – Leela Chander, Seetha Muthiah Venila Thiagarajan, Mahema & Manohar Devadoss for sharing their recipes – Ram Gopala krishnan for his unstinted support throughout, helping with the computer, the prinouts and drawings.

About the Author

I belong to a Tamilian community where food is rated very high. Born and brought up in Bangalore and living in a family which observed convention as well as some principles of modernity, I learnt to respect food as being something precious, and definitely not to be wasted. I still have childhood memories of the number of people my parents hosted, the way they sat round our huge dining table, and how my father discussed the day's menu with my mother. As children we loved to ride with my father to Rusell Market for groceries, vegetables and meat for those special family get-togethers while the rest of the city slept. I remember the mounds of the family's favourite beans... *mochakka,* during the winter season.

Coffee making was an art... the coffee seeds were roasted and ground at home, to make just enough powder for the day. I can still close my eyes and recall the aroma of coffee being made in the coffee-filters, even though it was a banned drink for us as children!

My father, who was a doctor, did not believe in refrigeration. Cooked food was eaten piping hot and leftovers distributed to the hungry. Fresh food was always cooked in the evening for the night meal. Excepting my mother, our family was non-vegetarian, and my father personally shopped for the best of meat, chicken and fish. Cooking intrigued me, and I was fascinated at the amount of effort it took to produce a good meal. Early marriage and moving away from home prevented me from learning first-hand traditional receipes from my mother, though of course, she sent me recipes regularly by post, to far-away Bhopal where my husband and I lived. But the inputs I received as I grew up, remained with me through my adult life.

My inspiration to becoming a good cook was my husband, who apart from being an engineer has remarkable prowess in innovating and creating his own recipes. The exotic *chuppal* curry in this book is a 60-year-old speciality from his family, inspired by Persian friends and their cuisine. It was a challenge for me to keep up the family tradition of good food and I still remember glowing with happiness, when my mother-in-law certified that I was a good cook!

The tide of life took me to other areas of interest. I completed my M.A. in Sociology when my children started full time school. I was also an established textile and fashion designer in Madras, having introduced for the first time, the boutique concept in a tradition bound city. I got involved with the nitty gritty of creating trends, fashion shows, choreography, script writing and compering. I became known as a media person as I went whole hog into journalism both as a correspondent and freelancer for most of the leading newspapers and journals in the country. And then, television, as a hostess, presenter and script writer for national network programmes.

In all of this I just could not keep away from the kitchen, and my children and husband enjoyed whatever I could prepare in a short time. I found myself winning prizes in cookery competitions, or by just sending my own recipes to magazines. I was invited frequently to judge cookery competitions. But it was really the encouragement of friends and family who have eaten at our table that inspired me to get a cookbook going. While I specialised in non-conventional dishes, I found that traditional recipes were becoming scarce, and when some of the young girls in the family wanted them, the very people who could have provided the information had already passed on. I resolved to document these near languished recipes.

I began by collecting my mother's recipes, and moved on to collecting recipes from other Tamilian communities. Certain hard-   to-get ingredients can be effectively substituted. The present-day gadgets cut out wearisome hours of labour without compromising too much on the taste of the dish.

Today our family is, by choice, more vegetarian and I find that meat can be effectively substituted by vegetables, and this is undoubtedly more healthful. We have travelled extensively, and one of my delights is to dwell on the cuisine of each region of the world I visit, and connect it to the lifestyles of the people. And, of course, therein lies the urge to modify it to suit the Indian palate. And maybe my next book will do just that!

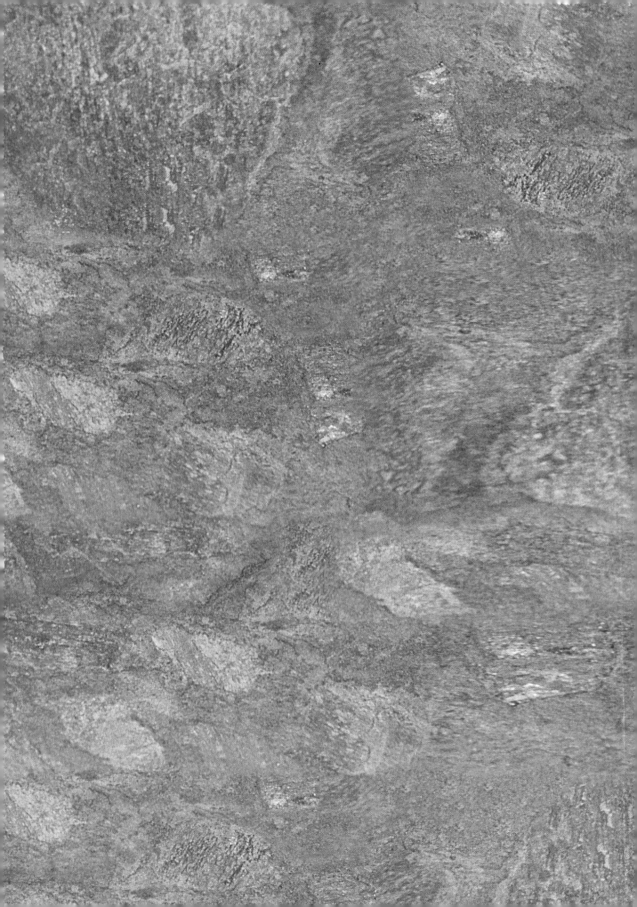